HIS SHOES HER SHOES
SOLE MATES
Marriage that lasts a lifetime.

Wayne & Tami Roberts

KAIO PUBLICATIONS, INC.

His Shoes Her Shoes: Sole Mates
Copyright © 2021 by Wayne & Tami Roberts
http://www.kaiopublications.org

All rights reserved. No part of this publication may be reproduced, stored in a retrieval system, or transmitted in any form by any means, electronic, mechanical, photocopy, recording, or otherwise, without the prior permission of the author, except as provided for by USA copyright law.

First printing 2021
Printed in the United States of America

ISBN: 978-1-952955-08-2

Grammar edited by Tonja McRady

Scripture quotations taken from the (NASB®) New American Standard Bible®, Copyright © 1960, 1971, 1977, 1995, 2020 by The Lockman Foundation. Used by permission. All rights reserved. www.lockman.org

Dedication

To our parents Emmett and Sue Roberts and Lyle and Bobbie Davison, who first showed us what faithfulness looks like in their faithfulness to God and to each other.

TABLE OF CONTENTS

Foreword iii

Introduction v

Chapter 1
Glass Slippers: Finding "Happily Ever After" 1

Chapter 2
Big Shoes to Fill: Being a Husband (From a Husband) 17

Chapter 3
These Shoes Are Too Tight: Being a Wife (From a Wife) 31

Chapter 4
Finding the "Perfect Fit": Making it Work 47

Chapter 5
"Hiking in High Heels": Being a Wife (From a Husband) 65

Chapter 6
These Shoes Are Too Big: Being a Husband (From a Wife) 81

Chapter 7
Tongue Tied: Improving Your Communication 99

Chapter 8
Shoeless: Intimacy in Marriage (From a Husband) 113

Chapter 9
The Fashion of Passion: Intimacy in Marriage (From a Wife) 127

Chapter 10
Keeping Your Shoes Shined: Faithfulness in Marriage 143

Chapter 11
It's All About Their Soles (Souls): Getting to Heaven... Together 155

FOREWORD

There are countless books on marriage, but you have never read anything more practical and fun than *Sole Mates* from the *His Shoes, Her Shoes* team of Wayne and Tami Roberts. Wayne is one of my favorite speakers. Now he brings his delightful style to the written page with soul-stirring insights on his favorite topic: making the most of your marriage. Wayne's wife Tami joins him in bringing a fresh feminine perspective to the topic of wedlock. Tami speaks with unmatched honesty and humor. Neither author holds anything back. As you read these pages, you will think, laugh, weep, and grow.

Wayne and Tami's philosophy is that marriage is best when two people approach it with deep consideration for each other's feelings and needs. This book will help you master the art of empathy, the key skill for success in marriage. The magic begins the moment you commit to walking daily in your mate's shoes. There is no other way to understand his mind or to win her heart.

This work is not a collection of rehashed platitudes. It treats readers honestly and respectfully. No difficult topic is dodged, and no thorny issue is sugarcoated. In this book you will learn the importance of electronic faithfulness. You will become proficient in speaking a whole new language. Best of all, you will discover the joy of being soul-mates by making every decision with the welfare of the other's soul in mind.

The Roberts' unique style makes this book fun, but the biblical foundation makes it priceless. The authors write, "Marriage is all about the soul, and your soul has a lot to do with your marriage." The fact is that you will never understand marriage rightly until you view it from a soul perspective. The perfect fit has less to do with finding the perfect partner than with being formed more perfectly into the image of Christ.

Sole Mates is ideal for your Bible class or for personal study. It is a practical book designed to produce positive change in your marriage by producing spiritual change in you. Wayne and Tami urge readers not to settle for a happily **ever** after marriage when what you want is a happily **forever** after marriage. The authors set the mark high, but why not? They know that you can do anything with the right shoes!

- Aubrey Johnson, Author of *The Best Husband Ever*
and *Consider One Another*

INTRODUCTION

Tami and I have five children (I started to say grown children, but that's yet to be seen). Our oldest child is 40. Our youngest is now 30. It seems like we had one every year in between. We were so thankful when somebody said, "You know, when God told Adam and Eve to replenish the earth, that other people are helping with that." Such a relief. Anyway, we had a houseful. So, we had a very regimented evening. When school time was over, they came home and there were chores to do. Then there was homework. Then we had dinner, cleaned up, had a little bit of play time, a little television time, wrapped up the chores, wrapped up the homework, and finally started bedtime about 8:30.

Many of you who are parents know that there is an 8:30 bedtime...and a 9:30 bedtime...and a 10:00 bedtime. Finally, about 10 o'clock everybody would be settled (or, at least, afraid for their lives), and they were quiet. Tami would go off at 10 o'clock for one hour almost to the minute to take a bath. It was just her personal private time. It's quiet, and I didn't bother her. She sang, she laughed, she cried, or she read. I don't know what all went on in there. It was up to her. I just would catch up on all of my movies and television programs for that hour. Then she would come in about 11 o'clock, and we would sit down and visit for a little bit, maybe play a game or just watch some television. And then, midnight would strike, and we would think, *"Hey, it's a whole new day, maybe we ought to get up and go to bed and be ready for it."*

Well, the kids have now moved out, but the process stays about the same. At about 10 o'clock, Tami goes off to take her bath, comes in about 11, and we'll sit some nights watching the clock. "57, 58, 59, it's midnight, let's go to bed." We are just creatures of habit, I guess. But one night, I was so tired, I just couldn't stay awake. I had already taken like three naps on the couch, and Tami came out from her bath to sit with me and visit. I said, "Honey, I'm sorry, but I have to go to bed." And she said, "Well, I'm not ready for bed yet." But we've always, with the exception of maybe a unique circumstance or sickness, gone to bed at the same time. "I'll go to bed," she said, "but I'm going to sit up and read." This doesn't bother me. I have these little shutters (eyelids), and when I close them, it's "Good night, sweet prince." I will say, though, that for Tami, her process is a bit more elaborate. I don't want to share family secrets, but when she takes her bath, out come her contact lenses, and on goes this pair of glasses that looks like she got them in the third grade. She has been trying to keep up with me in age, however, and those glasses are not enough for her eyes, so she has a pair of reading glasses which she perches on the end of her nose…in front of the other glasses. She's also in a phase of life where she comes out of the bath and is so hot that she puts on a flannel PJ top to keep from getting too cold. Please don't ask me to explain. It's just the way that it is.

So Tami climbed in bed, wearing two pairs of glasses, a flannel pajama top, a book as big as a dictionary (something about fairies chasing unicorns) with a book light on it. Her hair was kind of curly from the steam of the bath. I was already half asleep when she turned to me, kissed me, and said, "I love you. Sleep good." I kind of mumbled back, "You too," and with the half-opened eye that was not buried in the pillow, I looked up at her and thought, *"That is, without a doubt, the goofiest looking gal I have ever seen in my life. But I'm glad that she's my gal. I'm glad she's my wife. I'm glad she's the mother of my children and the grandmother to my grandchildren. I'm glad that she intersected my life and became part of my story."* And that's when an epiphany came. What if it isn't that she is **my** wife? What if she isn't mother to **my** children or she isn't grandmother to **my** grandchildren? What if she didn't intersect **my** life and become part of **my** story? Rather what if I'm **her** husband—and father to **her** children and the grandfather to **her** grandchildren? What if, in fact, I have intersected **her** life and become part of **her** story?

I got up the next morning and apologized to her and said, "For over 30 years now I have been looking at our marriage from my perspective." I told her, "I'm going to do the best I can with the time that God gives me to look at our marriage from your perspective, from your shoes." It wasn't that we didn't have a good marriage, that we didn't interact, that she wasn't a part of it; but I had been thinking about our marriage in terms of my hopes, my dreams, and what I wanted out of it. I hadn't taken enough time to think about what our marriage looks like from her perspective. It was a new view of our relationship. It was a perspective we hadn't really had before. It was an approach to our marriage that made such a dramatic difference that we felt we had to share it with others. That's where this material got its start. Then it became a single seminar at the congregation where we were working. In 2013 it became the *His Shoes, Her Shoes* marriage seminar.

Song of Solomon 1:4 says, "Come, let us run away together." That's what we what to encourage you to do as you go through this material—run away **together** and to do so in each other's shoes. As the old adage goes, "If you walk a mile in someone else's shoes, you have a better understanding of them." We want you to finish this book with a greater appreciation for your spouse and the role that he or she has in your marriage. It won't fix all of your problems. You've spent years making that mess. No book can clean it up that quickly. However, we do believe that the perspective we'll share will help—if your marriage is struggling—to work your way out of some of those problems. And if you're kicking back saying, "You know what, our marriage is just fine," the perspective we want to share will help you move from a "just fine" marriage to a thriving marriage. It's not going to be for any one unique group of people or any one particular kind of marriage. There will be something for every married couple (and for the unmarried folks as well). No matter what condition your marriage is in, we invite you at least to give it a consideration. We want your marriage to be better than it is today. Tami and I do not come with any qualifications other than almost 40 years of marriage and a number of mistakes, some of which we will share along the way. So, grab your shoes. Here we go!

CHAPTER 1

GLASS SLIPPERS: FINDING "HAPPILY EVER AFTER"

When Tami and I started the marriage seminar, we said, "Okay, what are we going to share in our marriage seminar that hasn't already been shared before?" We decided first of all we wanted to make sure that whatever we had to share was not just from our experience, but first and foremost from that which we have confidence in: namely, the things that God shares in His Word. The perspective we share is prayerfully always from God's perspective, though we will show you in many illustrations times when we went awry from that. Hopefully you will have an opportunity to learn the easy way rather than learning in some of the ways that we did.

The next thing we decided was that we didn't just want to regurgitate stuff that everybody has already heard. I mean, there are all kinds of good marriage books that all discuss the same topics. However, there are also some fundamental principles we decided could not be skirted even if everyone already knew them. Remember in college you had to go through some of those beginner classes like English. Everyone thought, "*I already speak English; I don't need to take English.*" However, when I took English, I found out that what I spoke wasn't actually considered English (so now I'm bilingual, I guess). We realized that, before we could lay down any new foundation, there were some things that needed to be untangled. Some things needed to be discarded—a series of misconceptions people often have about marriage that we believe are contributing to a lot of the marriage problems that exist. Some couples have ideas and beliefs about what marriage should be, even though that's not at all what it should be. When those expectations are not met (because they never could be met), people get disappointed, they get discouraged, and they even get divorced. So, we need to work through a few of those ideas before we can start laying out some new ideas.

The misconception that some have about marriage can be illustrated best in a little French short story called "The Glass Slipper." You know it better as Cinderella. We all know Cinderella's story, right? Here's the way it goes: Cinderella was raised by her ugly stepmother and her ugly stepsisters. She was mistreated; she was the maid, the laundry woman, and the cook. She had nothing. Word came from the palace that the handsome prince was going to hold a big ball and he planned to invite all the eligible ladies of the kingdom. From these, he would select a wife for himself. The ugly stepmother, seeing an opportunity for a husband, put on her very best. The ugly stepsisters, also eager for mates, put on their very best. They were about to go out the door, and down came Cinderella. She was pulling her rags up on her, and they said, "Where do you think you're going?" She said, "I'm going to the fancy ball along with you." And they said, "No, you're not! He wouldn't want anything to do with you." And off they went.

Cinderella stayed behind, crying. Next thing you know, something happened! Her fairy godmother showed up. A little bippity, a little boppity, a little boo, and all of a sudden, fantastic things were happening. I mean, her clothes turned into a beautiful gown, squirrels and rabbits helped her dress, rats became coachmen, and then, of course, a pumpkin became a carriage in which she could ride.

Just before she left, the Fairy Godmother had two more things to do. First, she slipped a beautiful pair of glass slippers on Cinderella's feet. Next, she said, "You'd better be home before the last stroke of midnight, because then everything goes back to the way it was." I mean, what would a fairy tale be without a curfew? So off they went, up the mountain, and she arrived at the fancy ball. She walked in, and she caught the prince's eye and vice versa. They danced all night, much to the chagrin of everybody there. But then she heard it: *Bong...bong...bong*. It was midnight and she knew what would happen on the last stroke. Out of the prince's arms and out of the ballroom she ran, down the stairs heading for her carriage, and she ran so fast she ran right out of one of those glass slippers. She jumped into her carriage and headed for home. There's a side of me that always wondered what would have happened if she had just missed it by a little bit and had still been inside the carriage when it changed back into a pumpkin. But back to our story. All she left behind was a beautiful memory and that one slipper. When the prince found it, he announced, "Whoever fits in this glass slipper will be my bride." Apparently there was only one size 6-and-a-half in the whole kingdom. So off he went from village to village, from cottage to cottage. No success. Finally, he arrived at Cinderella's house. He tried it on the stepmother; no, it didn't fit. He tried it on the stepsisters; no, it didn't fit. Then he tried it on Cinderella. It fit and... everyone say it together... "*They live happily ever after.*" And that's just the way it is in real life...right?

Let me just tell you what I think about that glass slipper. I don't like feet. It's one of those questions I want to ask God: "When You created feet, what were You thinking?" I imagine that I can see Cinderella's ugly feet through those glass slippers. I say ugly because she's been living a pretty impoverished lifestyle. I bet she never had a pedicure. She had those nasty, dirty feet with gnarly toenails shoved down in that shoe. Of course, as she begins walking, they would start to perspire. So now there's these sweaty feet inside of them. And the story never says it, but I think on the top of her toe was one curly, ugly, black hair. This is not much of a fairy tale as far as I'm concerned. But rarely do young ladies see the reality that lies behind the fairy tale. Their marriages are set up to be a disappointment.

The situation isn't much different for young men. You know what Walt Disney and Hugh Hefner have in common? No. Not bunnies. Hugh Hefner, the creator of the so-called Playboy empire, and Walt Disney, with all of his fanciful retellings of wonderful fairy tales, have this in common: both of them paint an unrealistic view of love, romance, and the relationship between a man and a woman. Obviously, Hefner's pornographic story is far more vulgar and obscene than Disney's fantasy, but both present a lie about what marriage should look like.

There are young women who buy into what Disney tells them about how a marriage looks, and many young men who buy into what Hefner says about the relationship between a man and a woman. Then, when they get into the marriage relationship and find out that these perceptions were unrealistic, they become disappointed and disillusioned. But the problem is not the marriage; the problem is the baggage they brought into that marriage. Honestly, the misconceptions that many people have about marriage are just as ugly as the foot I just described earlier. We need to see the glass-slippered misconceptions painted by Hollywood, the media, and society for what they are: ugly. Let's see if we can't reveal a few of those misconceptions.

EXTERNAL BEAUTY IS MOST IMPORTANT.

If you are married, think back to the first time you saw your spouse-to-be. There was something physically attractive! I mean, some of you ladies may have said, "You know what, I think it would be really honorable for me to find the ugliest guy I can and then marry him." But I doubt it. People look for beauty! I mean, millions of dollars are spent every year in the pursuit of beauty. Ladies, you'll understand this: Picture the little mermaid Ariel and how her hair always looks great—even wet! It's not that way in real life, right? The idea is that we try to cultivate our external beauty, preserve our external beauty, and show off our external beauty because we feel it is what is most important. Oh yeah, we also often look for external beauty. We find that the thing that we're most in love with is the external beauty. Then one night we go to bed with this beautiful fantasy, and we wake up with the ogre Shrek. I understand that some of you women may have had a similar experience (wink).

Tami and I were in Beverly Hills about a year ago, walking down Rodeo Drive. There were some ladies who walked by us thinking that they had preserved external beauty forever. Picture faces stretched so far back that their pigtails were now a single ponytail. They hadn't preserved it, only prolonged the inevitable. Here's the truth: external beauty always, **always** fades. Skin wrinkles. Hair turns gray or falls out. We stay in shape, because round is still a shape. Youth doesn't last. So does the world's view of beauty. **Always**! External beauty however is not what ultimately matters. It is the person inside, the character of a person who we ultimately should be in love with, who we ultimately should be seeking. Many of us have stood by the casket of a loved one and looked at the body that we recognize externally and thought, *"That is not him. That's just his body."* We forget that sometimes when it come to our marriage relationship. For those who aren't yet married, it is that inside person you need to be spending the greatest amount of time in preparing and getting ready for marriage and what you need to be looking for in a spouse. Character counts **big**!

THERE IS SUCH A THING AS A PERFECT MATE.

"She is perfect." "He is perfect." "We just perfect together." You've heard this before from young dating couples, right? "It's destiny…We belong together…It's written in the stars…We are meant to be together." That is unless they find somebody else with whom they are "destined" to be. And don't forget, "I've found my soulmate!" Let me just say this, the only real "soulmate" is the person whose greatest interest is your soul. But we'll talk more about that later. It's the idea that this is all planned by God. And when someone comes along and says, "You know what, you don't belong together," it just fuels the fire. They believe that it's like Romeo and Juliet. Their parents hated each other, and it just proved they belonged together. I remind them how it turned out for Romeo and Juliet—not so good.

I only know of one divinely pre-arranged marriage in all of human history: Adam and Eve. Picture it this way: Adam's still trying to figure things out. He comes up one day, and says, "Hey, Eve, I wonder if you love me." And she turns back and says, "Of course I do, silly. I mean…who else?" That's the only pre-arranged marriage that there has ever been.

I'm not talking about God's providence and His answers to prayers. I certainly think that He not only answered my prayers, but He also said, "Here are some things you should have been praying for. I'll answer those, too." But I can tell you this: I did not marry Tami because she was "the one." Tami is **the one** because she's the one I chose to marry. That's the difference. God may be working, but for the most part He lets us choose our spouses.

We look to find the perfect mate, then we find and marry people who we think are the perfect mates. Then one day we discover that they are not perfect, and we might question if they are our perfect mates and look for another "perfect mate." It's a vicious misconception that can never be satisfied. Furthermore, if there was such thing as a "perfect" mate, most of us would be single because we are all imperfect in some way.

WE WILL HAVE NO PROBLEMS.

There will be no conflict, no difficulty, or no stress. It will be endless excitement and intimacy. Feel free to snicker here if you've been married longer than about 3 days. We see this misconception carried into a lot of marriages. "The honeymoon's over," people say when they begin to experience problems. Maybe it's him, maybe it's her, or maybe it's **us**. "Maybe we don't belong together, because in marriage we're not supposed to have any problems." Ridiculous, and yet somewhere in the back of our minds is this idea that if we're having problems, then there's something wrong with our spouses, or there's something wrong with our marriages... and we need to move on. Tami and I once coached a couple that had a fight the first night of their honeymoon and she locked him out of the hotel room for the entire night. He had to sleep on the beach. Now for some of you, sleeping on the beach may sound wonderful. It's not when you are alone and on your honeymoon. That couple continued to have problems and the misconception that marriages don't have problems contributed greatly to those problems.

This is an unrealistic expectation using logic alone. We live in a fallen world. It is a world that has been corrupted and polluted by sin! It once was perfect at one time, but it isn't anymore. None of this will change just because you get married. Good married people still have flat tires. And those who love each other, who are working together and trying to be godly, sometimes they still get sick. They lose their jobs, and it rains, and it snows. You can't drive down the streets of Denver in the cold, snowy months of winter and say, "That family must be having a wonderful marriage, because, look! The snow doesn't stick on their driveway." It isn't realistic to believe that. There will be times in which there is some unhappiness in your marriage. There may be some time in which loneliness is felt, and perhaps even times in which you or your spouse will feel unsatisfied. But that does not mean that the marriage is not what it's supposed to be.

Listen carefully (I won't say, "If there's any one thing you need to take away it's this," but, honestly, this is a pretty good one): Every single marriage has problems! Anybody who tells you that his or her marriage doesn't have problems has a problem—somebody in that marriage is a liar! Because every marriage has problems. And, although I don't know what problems you might face in your relationship, I can all but guarantee you this: someone, somewhere, has a bigger problem than your problem, but he or she is working his or her way through it with God's help. That should be good news for you, whatever your problem is! I know what you're thinking, "Yeah, but my problem really is bigger." Well, the only reason it seems bigger is because it's **your** problem. Every marriage has problems, and there are opportunities for every marriage to work through those problems if we seek God's help. We will discuss this in depth later.

MARRIAGE IS EASY!

People often think, *"It really doesn't take any work at all and if, at any point in time, it takes a little bit of blood, sweat, and tears for our marriage to work—it's just not worth it because it's not supposed to be hard work."* They think, *"If it takes any work, then it must not have been meant to be. Because marriage is easy. It's supposed to happen naturally. We'll fit together perfectly. We'll never steal the sheets from one another. There will never be dirty underwear left on the floor. It will all work together just like...magic!"*

This may be revolutionary for some (write this one down): There is no such thing as magic. Okay? You don't just bippity-boppity-boo your way through marriage. Some people say, "Marriage is 50/50." That's not true. Divorce is 50/50. I used to say that it took 110% on the part of each spouse to make it work. A friend changed my mind on this. She says that marriage somedays is 20/35 and you pull your 55% together, put on your big boy (or girl) pants and get to work with whatever you can muster. Sometimes it takes everything you both have, even for day-to-day life.

There is nothing of any value that has not had some level of work associated with it. That's part of what makes it so special. If it were easy, it would be almost commonplace. People would think, *"What's the big deal? Everybody has a perfect marriage."* But in reality, it requires working together and finding a way through it! I've had a hard time fully explaining this to my own kids much less to people in our seminars. The work is worth it! Take for example folks who climb the world's tallest mountain Mt. Everest. They helicopter in to a base camp, cross a rocky field, tiptoe over a deep chasm on an aluminum ladder bridge, navigate a glacier, scale the sheer face of the peak, and pass dozens of bodies of those who failed in their trek frozen in the snow as they make their accent. Finally, with the temperature and oxygen level dropping, they reach the summit. The very top of the world. I can't imagine any of them saying, "Huh. Is that it? Not sure it was worth it." It was worth it, in spite of all of the work. That's why many of them go back time and time again. It's the same with our marriages: What lies on the other side of the work is worth it. Trust me. The great thing is that whether you're at 10% or 110%, God helps make up the difference if we put our trust in Him. You don't have to face the challenges alone.

QUALITY TIME IS MORE IMPORTANT THAN THE QUANTITY OF TIME.

Married couples can think that what makes a marriage special is all the special occasions. First there is the wedding day, then the honeymoon, then birthdays, vacations, holidays, anniversaries, second honeymoons, etc. They need a constant stream of "special" days to keep the marriage special. It becomes about all the special occasions.

I'm reminded of a story about a guy who grabbed a handful of bacon and some coffee as he headed out the door (obviously, on a low-carb diet). He kissed his wife on the forehead, and just as he got to the door she said, "Have a good day. You know what today is!" Those are unsettling words for a man...because he doesn't know what today is. And, it's not all his fault—you ladies have an anniversary for everything. You don't just have a birthday anniversary and a Valentine's Day anniversary and an Anniversary anniversary, but you have an anniversary for things like the first time both of you wore blue at the same time! So, the husband was thinking as he was driving to work, "*What is today?*" He looked in his day planner and there is nothing there. "*Oh boy, what is today? How could I forget?*" So, he calls and orders a dozen flowers and has a card put with them that says, "On this, our special day. Love, Me." He was feeling pretty good until he arrived at the office. Then he thinks, "Yeah, but I send that for the regular special occasions. What if this is one of the biggies?" Just to be safe he called the florist back and said, "Make that two dozen roses." He went about his work again. About mid-morning, it hit him. "Yeah, but I sent two dozen flowers to my mom on her birthday!" So he told the secretary, "Would you send a box of candy, a big box of candy, to my wife for me?" At lunch, he thought, "This might not be enough." He remembered that she liked a bracelet in the jewelry store, so he popped in and bought that little bracelet. Now he's all set.

By mid-afternoon he was second-guessing himself as we men do (even though we may not admit it). He called his wife to tell her that he was going to take her out to the fancy restaurant she had been wanting to go to for some time. She was out picking up the kids, so he left a really nice message, saying, "You be ready when I get home. We're going out on the town tonight. My parents are coming to get the kids." Everything was great until he was driving home, and he remembered, "No, wait a minute. The last time we were going to go there, she said that the place was too fancy, and that she didn't have anything to wear." So, off the highway he went, stopping into a little boutique to grab an appropriate outfit.

When he got home, there as he walked through the door he saw, fanned out like the NBC peacock, those two dozen roses, with that little card, "On this, our special day. Love, Me." He was feeling pretty good. The chocolate box was open (only one is gone, right, ladies? If he had turned them over, he'd have seen there was a hole in the bottom of all of them as she tried to figure out which was her favorite). Then, she walked into the room, glowing like the Madonna (not Madonna, but **the** Madonna) as he held that bracelet over his wrist.

Her eyes lit up, as he said, "I guess you got my phone message?" She said, "Oh, honey. I don't want to be a party pooper, but that place is too fancy." And he replied, "I know—you don't have anything to wear, do you?" When she said, "No," he ceremonially pulls the outfit he bought from its bag and exclaims, "You do now. Ta-dah!"

Then she said, "You are the best husband in the world, and this is without a doubt a Ground Hog Day I will never forget."

Now, guys, don't misunderstand: You still need to remember the special occasions (February 14 is Valentine's Day. Glad I could help). There is something about special days and the opportunity they provide for remembering and celebrating those anniversaries. But let me just tell you right now, they are not really any more important than the other days. I learned that a number of years ago. Tami had gotten up in the night, and I figured she was just on her way to the bathroom. Then, I heard a kind of *thud* in the bathroom. I found her lying on the floor. You know how it is when you have the flu and you don't want to go far from the bathroom? She had kind of postured herself on the floor that way… yet she was also up against the door, so I could hardly open it to see what had happened. So, through the door, I began asking if she was okay. But she didn't say anything. I asked her again, "Tam, are you okay?" Still nothing! I pushed my way into the bathroom. When I laid her head back, I saw her eyes had rolled back in her head and she was unresponsive. It seemed like years (though I'm sure now that it was only minutes) as dozens of thoughts ran through my head. *"Could this possibly be it? I mean, she's young! What will I tell her children and her grandchildren? This isn't the way it's supposed to be. What am I going to do from here on out?"* I had an aunt who had a similar situation. She had a cerebral aneurysm that ruptured in the night, and she died from it. I knew it could happen just that quickly, but I thought, *"It can't be happening now! How will I get to the phone? Should I scream for help and hope somebody hears me? How can I get the door unlocked so they could get into the house?"* All of these things raced through my mind. At the same time, I kept saying, "Tam, Tam, TAM!" Still no response.

Then suddenly, her eyes rolled back in her head like a Las Vegas slot machine, and she looked right at me and in a loving, caring voice said, **"What**? I hear you." Relieved, I asked her if she had seen Jesus. "Why?" she asked. "Because," I said, "I think I'm going to send you to Him. You about gave me a heart attack!" It turned out not to be anything serious. But in that moment, I realized that the days in between special occasions are just as important. What makes a day special, whether it's a good or a bad day, whether it's sunny or rainy, is that her shoes are next to my shoes. Those days that are the special days, and I am foolish to believe that "special days" are all that matter.

SEPARATION MAKES THINGS BETTER.

Now, let me just give one caveat with this: I understand that sometimes, when there are problems in a relationship, we need to go to our neutral corners to cool off a little bit. A moment of quiet between those warring parties may be necessary. I understand that in situations of abuse there is a need for a separation of physicality until some things are worked out. I even understand that God permits divorce (although it's not what He wants for us). But for the most part, separation does not make things better—it makes things worse.

It's been said, "Absence makes the heart grow fonder." What that really means is the farther away some people are, the more you like them. In other words, we can become quite used to the freedom of not having the responsibility of a spouse! But that does not help resolve problems. If you're a cat lover, I apologize in advance for this illustration: Sometimes married couples need to have their tails tied together and be thrown over the clothesline until they fight and get it worked out. This idea that separation, whether it's a "temporary" separation or a permanent one marked by divorce, frees you from problems is simply not true. It doesn't free you from problems; it just exchanges one set of problems for a new, different set of problems. May I suggest to you that those problems can permeate not only the husband and the wife and their relationship, but they are problems which plague other people around us (children, grandchildren, parents, grandparents, friends, neighbors, and relatives) in ways that maybe we've never considered.

THE PURPOSE OF MARRIAGE IS TO BE HAPPY.

This is probably the greatest misconception of all. This misconception involves the purpose of marriage. People get married for a variety of reasons. For love, for companionship, for money, or for the love and companionship of money. Some marry out of loneliness, and some, it would seem, out of boredom. Some marry for happiness and expect it to be **always happy.** They believe that in a good marriage, there will never be a time when they will be unhappy, lonely, or unfulfilled. They believe that marriage should characterized by, "And they lived happily ever after." There's no mention in those fairy tales whatsoever about the husband losing his job or a wife having to go to work. We don't have the stories about unexpected hardship and loss. Those stories just always end with "happily ever after." Then for these individuals, when unhappiness comes along (which on occasion it will), they are disappointed and disillusioned about their relationship. They believe they were promised **happily ever after**! They expect it, they pray for it, they may even demand it. Since in their minds marriage is all about happiness and they aren't happy, they begin to look for someone else who will make them "happy." They'll express their disappointment and decisions with statements like, "Well, God just wants me to be happy," or "Is it too much to just want to be happy?" Actually, it's too little to ask. Marriage is about far more than happiness.

Don't get me wrong. There isn't anything wrong with wanting a happy marriage, and certainly happiness is a product of a healthy marriage. However, making happiness the ultimate objective for marriage is like enjoying your favorite ice cream by just reading the ingredients on the carton. There is something much more satisfying. When we put happiness as the ultimate objective, I really believe God's response is, "That's it? I have so much more planned for your marriage!" Happiness, simply put, is settling in marriage. God has something more in store for you and your marriage than just happiness! He is more concerned about your holiness than He is about your happiness—because He has more planned than your "happily ever after." He's set on your "happily **forever** after."

At this point you might be thinking, "*Well, thank you so much, Wayne. I'm only one chapter into the book and you've told me that there is no such thing as a happily ever after.*" Well, there is, but it doesn't look anything like these misconceptions and the unrealistic expectations that some folks have.

Let me wrap this chapter up by showing you a snapshot of God's happily ever after. It's a happily ever that can be yours in your marriage. It is described nicely in the Song of Solomon (yes, that book that makes us blush). It begins in the very first chapter. It opens with a conversation between the bride and the groom-to-be. Note her words. She describes in Song of Solomon 1:2 what I call **genuine romantic love.** "May he kiss me with the kisses of his mouth, for your love is better than wine, your oils have a pleasing fragrance, your name is like purified oil."

It is figurative language, but here's what it means. Real romantic love has an element of physical attraction. "May he kiss me with the kisses of his mouth." You don't have to find somebody that is as ugly as stump and marry him or her. These two people were physically drawn to one another, and there's nothing wrong with that physical attraction.

But she goes on, "For your love is better than wine." That's an emotional statement. Real romantic love produces butterflies in the stomach, makes the mouth dry, puts a lump in the throat, and makes people stumble all over themselves. It's that ooey gooey feeling that we most often associate with love. It's okay to have an emotional draw to one another as well.

But the real thing that ties it all together is this, "Your name is like purified oil." The "name" speaks of character. This is the truly binding element of love. Because sometimes that physical attraction may falter and sometimes the emotional connection may not be the same, but when one prides himself on connecting to the person and her character, it can outlast all of those things.

God's happily ever after has to do with not only real, genuine love, but also a mutual affection for one another paired with individual humility. As the story goes on, Solomon and his future wife go back and forth with thoughts about each other and about themselves. Here are some of her thoughts about herself,

> How dark I am, but lovely, O daughters of Jerusalem, Like the tents of Kedar, Like the curtains of Solomon. Do not stare at me because I am swarthy, For the sun has burned me. My mother's sons were angry with me; They made me caretaker of the vineyards, But I have not taken care of my own vineyard. (Song of Solomon 1:5-6)

Wow—"swarthy!" I don't think that's a good thing. She didn't see herself as very attractive. Loosely translated she is saying, "I'm just a farm gal. I've worked in the fields. My skin is leathery from the sun. My hands, they're coarse from working in the vineyard." She continues, "Though I have given much attention to my family's garden, I have not given much attention to my own garden (my appearance). I'm not much."

Then her husband responds, "Most beautiful of women…. How beautiful you are, my darling. How beautiful you are! …Like a lily among the thorns" (Song of Solomon 1:8, 15; 2:1). That sounds much better, doesn't it? He saying, "What are you talking about? In a garden of maidens you are the fairest of them all." Now she counters, "No, no, you're the good-looking one." Back and forth they go. There's this mutual affection for one another, but it is paired with individual humility.

That doesn't mean people need to walk around saying, "I am swarthy, I am swarthy, I am swarthy," but it is important to foster an attitude that says, "How fortunate and blessed I am to have this prize!" This attitude of prizing one another should be both from the wife to the husband and the husband to the wife.

Another characteristic of God's happily ever after comes from my wife's favorite verse. In Song of Solomon 2:16 it says, "My beloved is mine, and I am his." Simply put, this communicates the intent to remain committed to one another. Commitment starts at the front and looks forward. It says, "We will," not just "I do." But the intent to remain committed is really only one half of the bookends. The other half is found at the very end of Song of Solomon. Solomon writes, "Put me like a seal over your heart" (Song of Solomon 8:6). He was speaking of the king's seal. Once he put his seal on something, no one had the right to break it. He goes on, "For love [that is, our love—WR] is as strong as death, many waters cannot quench love, nor will rivers overflow it. If a man were to give all the riches of his house for love, it would be utterly despised" (Song of Solomon 8:7). This was written by the man who was one of the most wealthy individuals in all of Scripture! He says, "There is nothing more important than love." So, while commitment looks forward, here the couple also looks back and sees the fulfillment of that commitment in the form of faithfulness.

What I have described is a genuine, romantic love along with this mutual affection, paired with individual humility, combined with an intent and a fulfilled commitment to stay together. Then, in that beautiful picture of faithfulness which, if you will, cashes the check that was written years before— this couple shows that it can be finished, this journey that they started. That is God's happily ever after.

CHAPTER 2

BIG SHOES TO FILL: BEING A HUSBAND (FROM A HUSBAND)

My dad was a preacher for 50 years. He was a preacher's preacher. If you don't know what a preacher's preacher is, he is the guy who will wear a tie in the shower. That's the kind of preacher my dad was. It seemed like he always wore dress shoes. He would come in at the end of the day and kick off his shoes—I specifically remember a pair of brown, wingtip, leather dress shoes. As a little boy I would put my feet in his shoes. They were so big! I would shuffle around the floor acting like I was Dad. I knew way back then that my dad had really big shoes to fill. But it was not until much later when I realized how big they really were and how hard they were to fill.

Flash forward about 20 years. Tami and I went out on our first date at the end of February 1981, and we married at the end of June that same year. With a simple "I do," my life changed dramatically. See when Tami and I first met, though I didn't know it at the time, she was pregnant, so when we got married I gained a wife and a six-month-old son. Not mine biologically, but all mine, nevertheless. A few weeks after we got married, we were living in a modest apartment. It was a Saturday morning, Tami was asleep next to me; of course, the sun was shining on her and she looked like an angel (sorry, I always get carried away when I think of her). My son was asleep in the other room. I remember it like it was yesterday. I woke up quickly, sat straight up in bed with beads of sweat running off my face, and it hit me: *"What have I done? I'm the husband. I'm the father. I'm the one that's supposed to be responsible for this family. Just a few months ago, I was a single guy, living with my parents—now I'm the man of the family!"*

Before I got married, I had been working for a large engineering company as a designer/draftsman and was making pretty good money for a single guy. I had a 1971 Plymouth Satellite that had a 318 police interceptor in it. The Satellite was a sister car to the much more popular Duster, but it was a sweet ride. When that baby went, it really went! I didn't have a car payment. My only recurring monthly payment was my car insurance. It was about $25 per month, if I remember correctly. I had money to spend on whatever I wanted. I had very few responsibilities. I was living the good life! Then, on that morning, I realized how much things changed when I said, "I do!" Of course, I was glad I had married her. It was a good life, but the responsibility was enormous. All of a sudden I realized how big my daddy's shoes really were.

Before we look at things from our wives' perspective, it's probably important for us to take a little stroll in our own shoes. Let's take a look at what kind of husband we need to be. Don't worry, I'm not going to beat you up. I know where you're coming from; I feel your pain. Whatever suggestions I make are not coming from some high and mighty position, with me saying, "Hello to all of you down there—if you only knew what I knew!" No, it's to say that I've been where you are.

God has put in our closet a number of "shoes" of responsibility. Let's take a trip through a husband's closet.

DRESS SHOES: THE SPIRITUAL LEADER

God slides these big shoes out in front of all the rest. I don't know about you, but when I grew up, we had three kinds of clothes. We had dress clothes, we had play clothes, and we had school clothes. You never let Momma find you playing in your school clothes, and you didn't go to church in your play clothes. I once got caught outside in my school clothes, and my mom said, "You're not supposed to be outside in those! Put on your play clothes." But my play clothes were last year's school clothes. Those were confusing times.

But for me, whenever I think of spiritual things, I think of the dress shoes that were part of my church clothes—those black, plastic-y, uncomfortable, never-do-anything-but-wear-them-to-church kind of shoes. But for me, they are the epitome of the big pair of shoes God has given us, saying, "You are the spiritual leader of your family."

Men, I do not know exactly why God decided to put you and me in the role of spiritual leaders. There are some schools of thought. One of them is the fact that, simply put, God created man first and then created woman, so man was given the right to be the head of the family. The apostle Paul points back a little bit to this, talking about the man being created first. It may be, as some suppose, that man was given the responsibility because it was the woman who ate of the forbidden tree first. There is some merit to that reason as well. F. LaGard Smith, in his excellent book entitled *Male Spiritual Leadership*, suggests that it may very well be because you and I are not inclined as men to be spiritual. I mean, ladies will organize ladies' class and ladies' days and ladies' retreats. We're trying to catch up with "Guys, Guns, Grub, and God Day." But it takes intentional action on our part. Smith thinks maybe it was God's way of saying, "I'm going to give them the headship responsibility to make them be the men they are supposed to be." Maybe that's true. I don't know exactly why He picked the way that He did, but He did. I am certain of this; He gave us the responsibility to be the spiritual head of our family.

In Genesis chapter 3, when man and woman sinned having eaten from the forbidden tree, God brought punishment upon them and consequences as well. These consequences would affect every married couple from then on. He looked at the wife and said, "Your desire shall be for your husband, and he shall rule over you" (Genesis 3:16). *Rule* is the same word used elsewhere for a king's rule over a kingdom. Before you get carried away with the idea of being the lord of your castle, you may want to hear what all of that entails. When we get to the New Testament, we see this principle again. In Ephesians 5, "For the husband is the head of the wife" (vs. 23). Furthermore, Paul writes to the church in Corinth (and to us as well), "But I want you to understand that Christ is the head of every man, and the **man is the head of the woman…**" (1 Corinthians 11:3). The God-directed headship of the husband in the marriage relationship cannot be argued.

I understand the instruction, but that doesn't mean I understand any better why God believes that I'm the man for the job. Here's why. I have a little confession. For me, it's a full-time job being responsible for **me** spiritually. To put me in charge of my family doesn't seem like the best idea. I struggle all the time, and I feel that I'm not always the best choice to be the spiritual leader. I realize all over again how enormous those shoes are that God has given me to fill as the spiritual leader. I have to be, first, the spiritual example.

On Judgment Day, my wife is going to give an account to God for what she's done both good and bad; but I've got this sneaking suspicion that's more than a sneaking suspicion that I'm going to give a double account. I'm going to be asked to account for what I have done to fulfill the responsibility I have been given as being the spiritual head of my family. I'm not going to be able to justify myself by saying, "Those shoes were just too big to fill." These are the most important and probably the biggest shoes that we as husbands have to fill.

But we're men, right? Not being able to do something doesn't keep us from trying. Watch YouTube and you'll see that. We suck in our guts, stick out our chests and put our feet in those big spiritual shoes, and off we go. But, like one of those late-night infomercials, God says, "Wait, there's more," and He slides out in front of us another pair of shoes.

WORK BOOTS: THE PROVIDER

Maybe you have special work boots—steel-toed, anti-static, high ankle boots. I found the most interesting pair of work boots I'd ever seen a while back in Texas. A guy came up to me and said, "You've never seen boots like these." On the bottom was this kind of fibrous pad—you know that green scrub pad that your wife has under the sink? Never mind, guys have no idea what cleaning supplies are under the sink. Nevertheless, she has a pad under there for scrubbing the pots and pans. It was like that. These boots were made for walking on asphalt shingles on an inclined roof, so the person wearing them wouldn't slide. Over time as they began to wear out, they could be peeled off. They were Velcroed on and easily replaced. I thought those were pretty fascinating shoes.

Look back again at Genesis 3. When Eve is told that her husband would rule over her, God then looked to her husband Adam and said, "You're not off the hook, either." He said, "You know how everything was planted and watered by Me for your provision. It didn't need to be weeded or attended and it flourished without you having to work for it?" (I'm paraphrasing). "It's not going to be that way anymore. By the sweat of your face, you will have to work for your food" (Genesis 3:17-20). And man was haltered with the shackles of work. The next time the alarm goes off telling you to get up and get ready for work, you can thank Adam.

In our world, there are a lot of women who work. Some women who have to work and there are some women who choose to work. There are some women who, by agreement or because of her expertise, are the primary "bread winner" for the family. But make no mistake: Even if she works to contribute, even if she contributes heavily or primarily, even if you're Mr. Mom at home and she's out earning all the money, it doesn't change your God-given responsibility as the provider.

Here's how big of a deal it is to God. When He spoke through Paul to the church in Thessalonica (and to us) He said, "If a man is not willing to work, then he is not to eat either" (2 Thessalonians 3:10). He wasn't talking about a man who had lost a job of no fault of his own, or a man who, despite trying, can't find a job, or a man who works but is having trouble making ends meet; he's talking about a lazy man. Paul adds to the instruction in 2 Timothy 5:8, "But if anyone does not provide for his own, and especially for those of his household, he has denied the faith and is worse than an unbeliever." Wow! That's pretty serious. God expects us as men to work.

Here's another little confession. I've not always been the best provider for my family. Just before Tami and I started dating she bought a brand new car. It was a Chevy Chevette. I know it wasn't much of a car, but it was new and it was hers. When we got married, she turned it over to me for my daily commute to work. It was the most economical of our two vehicles, so it made sense.

One day at work I was going to go out for lunch and get something to eat. I got to the parking lot to the spot where I had parked the Chevette, and it was gone. Somebody had stolen it. I called the police and gave them my name, a description of the car, and the license plate number. The officer informed me that the car had not been stolen, it had been repossessed. Apparently, "monthly" payments mean **every** month. We were at that place in life where sometimes we were robbing Peter to pay Paul and had run out of apostles. Well, we got the Chevette back. A blessing or a curse—you decide. Bottom line, I'm not always the best provider for my family. But God says, "You don't get to choose," and He slides those work boots back out in front of me.

Being the provider is not limited to just providing financially. We are called by God to provide for all of her needs, affection, conversation, support, and commitment. We are to provide for her financially, emotionally, sexually, and most importantly spiritually. Being the provider is a huge pair of shoes to fill. As husbands, we are to "nurture and cherish" our wives like we would our own bodies (Ephesians 5:29). Not sure I'm always very good at doing that either. Bottom line, I'm not always the best provider for my family. But God says, "You don't get to choose," and He slides those work boots in front of me…and you. But we're men. We suck in our guts, stick out our chests, put one foot in the Dress Shoe, one in the Work Boot, and say, "Off to work I go!" Then God says, "But wait, there's more."

COMBAT BOOTS: THE PROTECTOR

I suppose we've all gone through this ritual: You get a nudge in the night and your wife's alarmed voice saying, "There's someone in the house." I remember one night Tami and I were living in what I called the Prison Apartment. I called it that because I we had criminals on either side of us. This same conversation occurred. I responded to her concern, "Honey, I can see the front door from here and it's locked and chained…. We're on the third floor…. We don't have anything valuable to steal…. This apartment is so small that if somebody were in it, they'd be in bed with us…." But you and I both know we're not going to just talk our way out of it. If I wanted to go back to sleep, I had to get out of bed, reach underneath the bed for my courage and a flashlight with the 12 batteries in it, and walk around the apartment, saying something like, "I don't know how you got in here, but you would be well served to get out the same way you came in!" All the while I'm thinking in my head, *"I hope there's nobody in here."* Confession time again—I am a bit of a scaredy cat and not always the best protector. Nevertheless, we husbands are charged by God with being the protector of our families. Not just the protector of our property, but our wives and children.

God, through the apostle Peter, describes the relationship this way, "Husbands, live with your wives in an understanding way, as with a weaker vessel" (1 Peter 3:7). Weaker vessel? Did you hear that? You mean women are fragile and frail? Maybe there are some, but I know plenty who can hold their own. They don't need any man protecting them. When Peter calls the woman a weaker vessel, he's not saying she might break. Now, some wives may physically be in a condition that might be considered frail and fragile. Others may have wives with whom a person wouldn't want to tangle even on a bet. That's not what Peter is saying. Let me help you to understand what that expression means.

In Denver, they have a beautiful art museum. In fact, it's one of the premier art museums in the United States. In one particular exhibit hall, up on a pedestal, they have a ceramic vase (they call a "vaawz"). That vase has a glass case over it with an alarm on it. There's a big, burly guard who protects it whenever the museum is open. If you were to walk up to that vase, get past the guard and alarm, lift the case and knock it off its pedestal, do you know what would happen when it hit the floor? It would break. It is fragile, and it is frail. Now, as some say, "Down at the Wal-Mart," you might notice inside the front door around February that they have a big shelf of glass vases, all priced at $1.96 apiece. There is no guard, no alarm, and no pedestal. But, if you were to walk over to one of those and knock it off, do you know what would happen when it hit the floor? It would break. It's fragile and frail.

Peter's point is not that the wife is frail in her physical frame. It is the fact that the wife is to be prized. She is to be lifted up, and she is to be protected. She's a special "vaawz," not a common vase. God has given you and me the responsibility of being the protector of that prize. But it is not just to be her protector against the bump in the night. There are some other things from which we have to protect her.

Sometimes the greatest single enemy that a wife will ever face in her married life is a husband who should be her protector but becomes her adversary. This is the husband who, at parties, feels the need to publicly point out her bad cooking, citing the way she does or doesn't make gravy. He's the husband who complains to friends about what kind of a wife he could have gotten, but what he got instead. He's the husband who tells the children, "Oh, don't pay attention to Mommy; she's just being mean and angry." Maybe it is simply in the way he speaks to her. The greatest challenge we have in trying to protect our wives is protecting them from us.

There are some other adversaries. Tami called me one time (I shouldn't say one time—she called me three times in the same month), saying she'd had a flat tire. She asked if I could leave work and come fix it. I said, "Woman," (that's what I call her when I love her) "I am working hard. I am working hard to put bread on the table, food in the kids' mouths, and clothes in the closet. You think those four bald tires magically appeared on your car?" (That may have been the reason she'd had the three flat tires). *"Why are you calling me?"* I thought. It's because I am her protector. When she says, "Hey, there's something stuck in toilet that looks like a Lincoln Log, but I'm not sure that it's a Lincoln Log." I'm thinking, *"Why are you telling me?"* It's because I am the protector. When something is rattling in the garbage disposal, I come to help (though I do make sure that she's far away from the switch when I put my hand down in it). Because guess why? I am her protector. I'm the one that protects her from flat tires and clogged-up sinks and clogged-up drains and things that don't work. I am her knight in shining armor. I am her protector. You are the protector of your wife.

We may not be the best protector in the world, but God still says, "These Combat Boots are yours." Again, we put one foot in a Dress Shoe and one in a Work Boot, and we throw the Combat Boots over our shoulders like a Continental soldier, and off we march. And then God says, "But wait, there's more." **Really**?!?! You have to be kidding. What more am I responsible for?

NO-NAME SHOES: FRIEND AND COMPANION

He slides out what may be the most difficult pair of shoes we have to fill. In fact, I don't have a good shoe analogy for these, because I can't think of one that fully describes the role that we have as husbands to be the friend, the lover, and the companion to our wives. I don't know. Maybe magical elf shoes with bells on the end. Somebody once suggested to me, "Hey, make them flip-flops. You know, the kind you wear when you are on vacation, and everything's good." That's not a bad idea. One guy said, "Make them house slippers." I thought that might work until I gently suggested, "Tami, get me my house slippers." (It didn't go over so well. But let's just leave it there). I even had someone suggest dancing shoes. He said, "When we're gliding through life, gazing into each other's eyes and in perfect step." I told him that I don't dance. He said maybe that's a lesson in itself. Ouch! Let's move on. Whatever they look like, God has companion shoes for us. He has given us that responsibility. In that very same passage where Paul says, "Wives, be in subjection to your husbands" (Ephesians 5:22), he turns to husbands and says, "And husbands, love your wives..." (vs. 25). If there was ever a piece of punctuation that I wanted to buy, I would like it to put a period right there and stop that sentence. Because then I could play the card that every man tries to play when he doesn't know what loving that way means.

"Husbands, love your wives." *I do!*

"Husbands, love your wives." *I'll try.*

"Husbands, love your wives." *I'm doing my best, right?*

However, the sentence does not end there. It says, "Husbands, love your wives **as Christ loved the church**." Christ gave His own life for His bride, and that's what God expects from us. It's one thing to walk through a dark apartment or house with gun or flashlight in hand, ready to die for your wife if necessary. It's an entirely different commitment to **live** for her every single day. Back up a few verses now to verse 21, "Subject yourself to one another in the fear of Christ." It's not a role reversal here; he's saying is that your life as a married couple is to be spent serving one another. The principle of mutual submission should regulate and permeate all that you do.

The love of our wives—the kind of real love that's described here and elsewhere in Scripture—is the kind of love that empties oneself for the sake of another. It's a choosing love that has, at its heart, the well-being of another. It's the love of giving, not getting. It's the love of self-sacrifice. It is the love that outlasts feelings and outlasts outward appearance. God says this is the kind of heart that you need to have for your wife.

These are the shoes that God slides out for us to wear—a spiritual leader, a provider, a protector, and a loving companion. They are truly **huge** shoes to fill. This is when we say, "How in the world am I supposed to do this?" For me personally, there have been plenty of times when I have said to myself (and to God), "I don't have an answer for the problem that our family faces. I don't know the words. I can't fix this." Many months I have reached the end of the money before the end of the month. I find myself with my head in my hands. "What am I supposed to do?" I have a feeling that I'm not unique in those feelings. Some men think, *"I can't"* and others say, *"I won't"* and they walk away.

What we typically do is begin to beat ourselves up over the fact that we can't fill those shoes God has given. It's like when I first started preaching and I decided, "Well, my daddy had some really nice leather dress shoes. I should get me a pair." It didn't matter how much they were going to cost; I wanted a really nice pair. I went to one of the high-end shoe stores, and I told the salesman, "I want a pair of good leather shoes, leather-soled. I want them to last. I want them to look good." I put my foot up on the stool, he measured my foot, and then with a little smirk, this guy with a pencil-thin mustache looked down his judgmental nose and said, "Sir, we don't have anything in this store that is suitable for you."

You see, I wear a manly size 7 shoe. The reason I wear a size 7 shoe is that I have a size 6 ½ foot that goes inside of it. The fancy shoe store didn't have anything smaller than an 8. I then moved to a mall shoe store. I was greeted by an eager salesman with what I believed was that day's lunch dribbled down his tie. I went in, put my foot up on the stool, and was met with the same commentary on my diminutive foot. He said, "Uhhhh," somewhat puzzled as to what to do next. "We don't have anything here that is smaller than a size 8." I picked up my dignity, tiptoed out on my little ballerina feet, and went over to one of the department store. I walked up to the young guy half my age and put my foot up on the stool pointing to a pair of shoes on the shelf I was interested in. He exclaimed, "**Wow**! Sir, we don't..." and I finished the sentence, "...have anything smaller than an 8?" As if I couldn't feel any worse, he said as I was getting up from the chair, "Have you tried our Big Boys' department?" Fully frustrated, I defiantly plopped back down in the chair and said, "I will tell you what you need to do. This shoe that I just picked out? I want you to get me a size 8. When you come back out here, you're going to put them on my feet, and you're going to point me to the hardware department." He said, "Why?" "Because," I replied, "when I get there, I'm going to find a big hammer and beat my feet until they swell to fit. Because I'm leaving here with new shoes."

That's what we do when we think we can't be all that we're supposed to be. We beat ourselves up, and we think we're going to make up the difference by swelling to fit the big shoes that God has given us. Or, even worse we just walk away…barefooted. I used to tell men (and myself), "Man up! It doesn't matter if you don't think you can do it, you're going to have do it anyway." At one seminar following that charge, a friend who was attending came up and told me, "Wayne, you have missed the important passage about the very thing you're talking about. It's Ephesians chapter 5:18." I looked and said, "That's not about marriage. That's the one about the use of alcohol." It reads, "Do not get drunk with wine, for that is a dissipation, but be filled with the Spirit." He replied, "That's your answer!" I thought about it for a little bit, and he's right. It's not about some miraculous indwelling (or "in-swelling"). It's not about some epiphany that we have. It's that God is there to help us fill the shoes that we can't fill by ourselves.

Here's how it works. God says, "I want you to be the spiritual leader of your family." And you say, "I can't." He responds, "How about I lead, you follow Me, they follow you, and I let you take the credit for being the spiritual leader?" In other words, to be the best spiritual leader, you be the best follower of God that you can and let them follow you. God knows where He's going, where we should be going, how to get there, and even where the dangers are. He's a perfect leader. We don't have to lead on our own. He's there too.

He says, "I need you to be the spiritual provider for your family." And you say, "Well, I can't." God says, "You're right; you can't. You can't provide the way that I can." When apostle Paul said to the Philippian church, "I can do all things through Christ who strengthens me" (Philippians 4:13), he didn't mean that he could lift a car. You know how I know that? They didn't have cars back then (insert laugh here). Anyway, he wasn't saying that he had unmeasured strength. He was saying that he, with God's help, could do whatever God asks him to do. Otherwise, God wouldn't ask him to do it. God never asks us to do what we cannot do, with His help. He continues in verse 19, "And my God shall supply all of your needs." Translation: "I do what God asks me to do, and He takes care of the rest." You might say, "But He can't pay the rent." Don't limit God on what He can do. He is in possession of and controls everything. He created the world with just the power of His voice; I think He can handle your needs." You be the man you're supposed to be, and let God take care of the rest." He's a perfect provider. We don't have to provide on our own. He's there too.

He says, "I want you to be the protector of your family." You say, "I can't." He says, "You're partially right, because even if you protected them from every adversary, every stopped-up drain, every flat tire, they still have two major enemies: sin and death. And you can't do a thing about that. But I can…and I did when I gave My Son." He's a perfect protector. We don't have to protect on our own. He's there too.

Here's where you might say, "Okay. I know what the last one is: friend, lover, companion. God are you going to make me the greatest lover in the world?" God says, "I am. I'm going to show you in the person of My Son, Jesus Christ, the greatest love that has ever been known. You love like He did, and you'll become the greatest lover." God says, "I help you fill your shoes."

When I walked into my junior year in high school a towering 4' 11". The girls do not flock around 4' 11" except to squat down and say, "Look, he's so cute." That was disheartening. I went home, and said, "You know, if I were only 'man-size,' life would be different. I mean, at least 5' tall would be great!" So, I did something about it. I took a piece of balsa wood I used for model making and carved two inserts for my shoes. I put them in my shoes, and the next morning I walked into that high school 5' ⅛" tall. 7 feet wouldn't have been any taller as far as I was concerned. I just needed a lift.

That's what God is saying: "How about I give you a little lift? When you can't, I can. When you depend on Me, I will. And you won't be disappointed." The reason why I think this is important is because we have this enormous weight to shoulder (and sometimes an enormous ego to go with it). We have those mornings where we wonder, what have we done? When we think to ourselves, "If I don't work, we don't eat. If I don't protect, we're in danger. If I don't lead, we're all lost. So much rests on me; so much is counting on me. I can't do this!" God reminds us, "I can, if you'll let Me help you with it."

This is so important—not just because we're men and God's given us a challenge, but for another reason. There's a good chance that your wife is in love with another man. Yup! It may be the man that you pretended to be when you first met her. Do you remember that man? The man who called her sweetheart all the time and never said anything gruff, bought her flowers, went to eat where she wanted to eat, and sat and listened to her mother go on and on and on? He's the one that came up to her and said, "Would you marry me?" And she said, "Well, of course I will!"

Or it may be that she's in love with the man that you promised you'd be. Remember that guy? The one who stood up in front of that auditorium full of people and the preacher and God and everybody? (My allergies were terrible that day—I mean, tears were welling up in my eyes). The preacher looked over and said, "Do you promise to love, to honor, to cherish, in sickness and health, in rich and poor, in good times and bad times, keeping yourself from all others, only for her?" Then he turned to her and said, "Will you marry him?" And she said, "I do. Who wouldn't? Didn't you hear what he said?"

Maybe she's in love with the man who she believes you ultimately will be. So often our wives see our potential even better than we do and are patiently waiting for those men to bloom. Tami shares this story to make my point. She was unmarried and pregnant. She had not yet revealed it to her friends, her family, or her church. She and I were not yet dating. She was attending church on a Wednesday night. I was speaking that night in a brief devotional that I like to call "Stumbling Through Psalm 23," because that's just what it was. It took me 50 years before I came close to understanding the value in "laying down in green pastures." But on that particular night, seeing all 126 pounds of me struggling through Scripture, she leaned over to a friend and said, "I could marry that guy." No, she had not lost her mind. She did marry me. And she waited through all those difficult years, until one day I came to her and said, "I'm ready to do what I think I was always supposed to be doing, and that is to go into full-time ministry." She said, "I've been waiting. I knew you were a preacher that night I heard you speak. I've just been waiting for you to know it as well." You see, she is in love with the man that I am growing, hopefully, to be.

Or maybe it is simply that your wife is in love with the man you have to be, the one you must be, the one you are called to be, the one God desires each of us to be. That's the one who she is in love with most. And she deserves that man. She deserves the one she is in love with, the one way back then who behaved the way he did, the one who promised the things he promised, the one who's trying to be all that he can be, and ultimately the one who is seeking not only to be pleasing to her, but to be pleasing to God as well.

The role God has given us as husbands is enormous. It is impossible when we just give it the casual pursuit. As we fill one pair of shoes, we realize we have forgotten another pair. We race over to it, and we try to fulfill both. Then we think, *"Oh, wait, there's another pair!"* They talk about women having shoes in their closets, but it is nothing compared to what we have in our closets with the shoes God has given us! But that doesn't give us an excuse not to wear them, if you will. We need to pray, "God help us be the men we must be, the men we're called to be, the men they need us to be, and the men You created us to be. Help us fill those shoes."

CHAPTER 3

THESE SHOES ARE TOO TIGHT: BEING A WIFE (FROM A WIFE)

As I share the topic of being a godly wife, my job is not to make you a list of the things you're doing wrong. We all have that list; I don't mean to add to it. I want to lift you up and let you know we all struggle and we all have our weak spots and our strong spots. It's going to be okay. Don't give up! We must realize that in our marriages, the only person that we can change is ourselves. I cannot change Wayne; that is not my role. My role as a Christian is to strive to be Christ-like. When I do that, then my marriage is blessed. For this lesson, I'm going to give a Biblical foundation for your role as the wife. I'm probably not going to share anything that you don't already know. We're women. Women get bombarded constantly with who we're supposed to be. Every ladies' class, every Ladies' Day, every study on women's role in the church—in all of these, we've been told about our role. You're just going to get it through Tami's filter and that can be interesting.

I can remember back when I first got married. I wanted to be a godly wife, a person who would be the woman she's supposed to be for her husband. I would go sit at the feet of godly women and feel overwhelmed. The role that they were painting and picturing for me was huge! You know those really tall, four-inch heel shoes—the ones with the pointy toes? They're really pretty. They look great sitting on the shelf, but when you put them on….ouch! When I would look at my role as a wife in those early years it made me feel like I was trying to climb mountains wearing those shoes. My shoes felt tight, and they hurt! It was a lot to take in.

My word is *striving*. *Striving* means you've got your eyes on the prize and that prize is to be like Jesus. We've got our eyes on Jesus, and we're doing what we can to be like Him. I'm not going to take my eye off of the focus. This doesn't mean I'm not going to mess up because I'm human—I'm not perfect.

The things I'm sharing are not just for newlyweds. Every one of us, in every stage, will need these reminders. We need to be reminded of what God has asked us to be and who He has called us to be. From the moment I said "I do," I committed myself not just to Wayne but to God. That has helped me in my walk and in my marriage, because there are days when I would like to kick Wayne out of the car going down the street—days when I don't like him. If you don't have those moments, I don't know who you are. You are Superwoman! I have those moments. When I'm in one of those moments, I remember, *"Wait, you promised God you would do stay and work through this. You made those promises to God, not just Wayne!"* It helps me change my thinking. I constantly remind myself that the only person in our marriage that I can change is myself. So, I am striving to be better, striving to be like Jesus.

As I share stories about myself, I want you to understand a couple of things. First, my married life is divided into two sections. The first section of our marriage is when Wayne was in heating and air-conditioning. The second section is the ministry part of our marriage. I will be making reference to those at different points. As I look back on happenings in my life, I have a clearer understanding of what was going on. When I'm in the moment, I'm clueless, but when I look back…then I get it!

One of the first aspects of our role as a godly wife is found back in the beginning. God creates Adam, and He brings all of the animals through for Adam to name. Adam is naming all of the animals, and Adam looked, but there was no one for him. And God said, "There's no one for Adam. I'm going to create a helper suitable for him" (Genesis 2:18).

God wanted a helper suitable for Adam, so He made a female. That's part of our role as the wife. You look at those ancient ladies' Bible class books and they use the word *helpmeet*. All it means is "a helper suitable" for him.

Before I understood what this really meant I would have told you that I married the wrong man. I felt that I couldn't be a "helper suitable" for Wayne. Let me explain. When Wayne and I got married, we were moving into our first apartment. Wayne was organizing his desk and had his top desk drawer with all these dividers in it, and everything had a place. His pencils were lined up in the desk drawer by length and also by color. He's very, very organized, and I was impressed with that.

I went into the bedroom and began unpacking my socks and underwear into my drawer in the dresser. Wayne walked in and saw me with my box, dumping my socks and underwear in the drawer, and he asked, "What are you doing?" I told him I was unpacking. "Aren't you going to fold those?" he asked. I said, "Who folds socks and underwear?" He replied that everyone did. "No," I said, "I don't fold socks and underwear." So, when I hear "helper suitable," I'm thinking, *"A helper suitable for him? No way. That is not me."* It is hard for me because our personalities are so different.

But ladies, we are "helpers suitable" for our husbands because we are females. That part we have without any effort. God knew that Adam needed a female, so He gave him Eve. Eve balanced out Adam. She helped him. We take our personality and use it in our relationship as one flesh (Ephesians 5:31) to work together for the best outcome for our marriage, our family. We've had to learn to communicate and talk to each other. Because the manner in which I balance him out, how I play the female role—the opposite of whatever role he is playing at the time—it changes along the way. In our marriage Wayne carries a lot of the "her needs," and I carry a lot of the "his needs," so we try to balance each other out. Everybody will play that role differently because we're all married to somebody different. Everybody's personality is different. You may be the "money manager" in your family. You may be more organized. We all know that in some areas we are "smarter" than our husbands. But be careful how you communicate that. You will figure out a way to balance him.

When we say "I do," part of the role we take on is to be submissive to our husbands. Now the first thing I needed was a definition for *submission* and this is the one that I was given: "to be obedient to; to put yourself under the authority of." Well, I'm telling you right now that my skin began to crawl with those words. Let me explain my personality for you. When I was born, I came out of the womb, looked up at my parents, and basically said, "You're not the boss of me. You are **not** the boss of me." I have been doing that all along my life journey. I was best friends with the principal in elementary school and junior high because we spent a lot of time together. I have this rebellious, independent spirit. Looking at my personality, this definition of *submission* made me think, "*Oh, this is going to be awful. This is just going to be awful!*"

I had to get in Scripture and ask, "Why do I do this?" It's because God asks it of me. Ephesians 5:22-24 says, "Wives, be subject to your own husbands as to the Lord; for the husband is the head of the wife as Christ also is the head of the church, He Himself being the Savior of the body. But as the church is subject to Christ, so also the wives ought to be to their husbands in everything." If you just pull out those two verses, the assumption is that God is just talking to women. But if you look up at verse 21 of Ephesians 5, He says, "And be subject to one another in the fear of Christ." We see in the picture God is painting that submission is something we all do, men and women. This is what Christianity is all about. It's about laying yourself aside for someone else. It's having the mind of Christ found in Philippians 2:3-4 where we "regard one another as more important than ourselves" and we "do not look out for our own personal interests, but also for the interest of others." Is it too much to ask to do that for the person that we love most?

The world has painted such an ugly picture of submission, slathering it all over us in the church. God says, "Whoa. That's not what I meant at all. It's something beautiful!" We need to think of it as something beautiful. As women, if we could do that, it would be easier to be submissive. It would be easier to put ourselves in that role. I'm trying—I really work to be submissive, but it can be hard, sometimes really hard. I know it doesn't come naturally for everybody, because we know in Titus 2:5, older women were told to teach the younger women to be subject to their own husbands. I was always so envious of those women for whom this seemed to be so easy. Find a woman that makes submission beautiful and talk to her about it. She can help you on your journey. It helps me to remember that submission is a gift that I give to Wayne not just because I love him, but because I'm striving to be Christ-like.

When we say "I do," part of the role we take on is to be respectful toward our husbands. In Ephesians 5:33, the very last verse in that chapter, it says, "Nevertheless, let each individual among you also love his own wife even as himself, and let the wife see to it that she respects her husband."

Respect is defined as having a high or special regard for, so we are to have a high or special regard for our husbands, to think highly of them. Now of course, it starts with how you even **think** about them. Fill your mind with positive thinking about your husband. Pray about it. Focus on his positive traits/characteristics.

I put several different aspects under the umbrella of respect. The first one is to be careful how you talk **about** your husband. I can remember back in the heating and air conditioning days a time when I would have some young women over for lunch after ladies' Bible class. We would be sitting around talking about our week and we would start sharing things about our husbands. Our intention was never to be ugly; we were just talking about life. We started sharing things like, "My husband—you will never believe this—he never, **never** wipes the toothpaste out of the sink." "Oh, well, my husband doesn't even **know** where the washer and dryer are." I had an older woman with us one day and she hung around to help me clean up after everyone left. As we were working she asked me, "Tami, when the girls left today, do you think they thought more highly of Wayne or do you think they thought less of him?" Well, I had no idea what she was talking about, so she clarified. "The things that you shared with the girls about Wayne today, do you think they left thinking more highly of him or do you think they thought less of him?" I told her that we weren't meaning to be ugly, that we were just talking about life, and she said that she understood and that she had done it as well. But she wanted me to just stop and think about the picture I had painted of my husband. I thought, "Yikes!" I did make him look bad with what I had shared. Now a few weeks later we were gathered for lunch again and the conversation rolled around to our husbands. It hit me, "*Oh, no.*" So, I decided to try something. I was just going to throw something positive into the conversation about Wayne and see what would happen.

I don't remember what it was, but I think it had something to do with his cooking. (My husband can outcook most women I know.) I threw it out there, saying, "Well, Wayne really made something wonderful for dinner this week..." and when I had finished you could see a hush kind of fall over the group. Suddenly, everyone started coming up with very different things to say. "Well, my husband, he mowed like he's never mowed before" and the one-upping each other resumed, this time about how great our husbands were. We need to remember that our words will disrespect or respect our husbands, and we always want to be lifting them up.

Also in the heating and air conditioning days, the kids were little and I would go in the summer and stay with my parents. One time I was at my mom and dad's, Wayne had called me and shared a decision that he had made, and I became really upset. I got off the phone, and I was crying. My dad was there, and I said, "Dad, you will not believe what he did." When I began relating the situation to my dad, he stopped me. My dad is a gentle, godly man. He said, "You won't ever talk about your husband to me that way. I don't care what he's done—he's a young man trying to do his best. The decision he made was not a sinful decision. You will not disrespect your husband to me." I cried even harder because now I was thinking, *"But you're my daddy!"* What a great lesson my dad taught me that day. He said, "You will respect that young man. He's trying. You will respect him."

It would be like your dog bringing something into the kitchen and spitting it out on the floor. That can be scary when you can't tell what it is. Here is something covered in dirt and appearing to be furry. You would get a broom and kind of poke it to figure out if it might still be alive. Then you discover that it was one of your favorite furry bedroom slippers that had been missing. It was one he'd chewed on, buried in the dirt, and brought back in, throwing his prize at your feet. How often do we do that with our words that we share about our husbands? We drag them through the mud, bury them in the dirt, and then spit them out at the feet of others. We need to make sure that the words that we share about our husbands lift them up. Make sure that we respect them with what we say about them.

We also want to be careful with how we talk **to** our husbands. We all know the lady that will stand in the foyer and speak harshly to her husband, "I told you to go get the car!" Then she turns to the group and says in front of him, "The man couldn't dress himself if it weren't for me." Yikes! I would never in my life turn to one of my best girlfriends and say, "I can't believe you wore your dirty shoes in the house! Can't you see I just mopped?" But I know words like that have come out of my mouth to my spouse. I would never talk to my friend that way, so why would I talk to my husband like that? We **must** be careful, ladies; that's disrespectful! We want to make sure that we are working to speak to our husbands in a respectful tone.

Part of learning to be respectful is that we need to learn to listen to our husbands. As women, we hear all the time, "Well, a woman needs to share so many words in a day, and her husband needs to learn to listen to her," not realizing that most of our husbands have no one else with whom they're going to talk about personal matters. Men don't do that. We do! We'll call a sister, a sister in Christ, our mom, a female just to share things. Our husbands don't do that. So sometimes we need to hush and let them talk, and listen to them, too, when they're needing to talk. That's part of being respectful as well.

Also, under the umbrella of respect is to make sure that you are doing what you can to build a life together. Remember, the "one flesh" aspect. I've seen so many marriages that the husband has his job, his friends, his life, and the wife has her job, her friends, her life, and they have very little to do with each other. This is a **huge** issue in marriages today! We live in a world that moves so fast. I know of couples that if you wanted to go out with them for dinner or something that you would have to call both of them because they never communicate. They each live their own lives and seldom compare calendars.

Marriages like these remind of a time I went shopping at Kohl's, and I wanted red shoes for the Christmas holidays. I found these cute, cute shoes. They had a little bow on them, they were satin, and they didn't have much of a heel so I thought, *"I would wear those!"* However, I am extremely cheap and no, it's not just because of having five children. I've always been that way. When I got married, my dad told me that I had a certain amount of money to spend on my wedding and what I didn't spend I could have. I saw that as a moneymaking moment. My cheapness actually can cause problems sometimes in my marriage. But anyway, I wasn't going to pay what they wanted for those shoes. I left. Then, I went back in the spring, and they were in the clearance section. I was pumped! (shoe term). I never find cute size 8 shoes on clearance. They were $10. I was so excited! They had my size. I put the right shoe on, looked in the mirror, and thought, *"I'm getting these."* But I went looking for the left shoe, and the other shoe in the box was...another right shoe. It was sad. I dug and I dug. Wayne and I decided that someone must actually have 2 left feet.

This is what it's like when people live in a marriage in which you live your life and he lives his life. Like those two red shoes, for two right feet—they looked like a pair of shoes in that box, but they weren't a functioning pair of shoes. So often we have a husband and wife in a home, but they aren't working to live one life. Out of respect we need to learn to live a life that is combined.

By the way, we can't control our husbands. We can't change them. Some of these things may have you thinking, *"Yeah, well, when he does, I will..."* We can only change ourselves. I am growing, I am striving to be like Jesus to bring glory to God, and Wayne will be benefitted by that. It really doesn't matter how Wayne is behaving. I still need to be who I am supposed to be to bring God glory.

Respecting my husband is something I am doing to glorify God, and Wayne benefits from my effort. For example, Wayne is a controller, so most of the time I let him think he's in control. Since I know this about him, out of respect to him, I've learned if I'm going to the grocery store and I decide that a 15-minute trip turns into a two-hour trip, no matter where he is, I send him a text and just let him know, "Hey, I'm going to be out a little while longer." I don't want him thinking I'm dead in the ditch somewhere. I know who he is and out of respect for him I communicate with him.

Another aspect of respecting our husbands involves the adage "Silence is golden." Silence is only golden when you are not intentionally being ugly. I talked with someone at church one day whose wife had been sick. I asked,

"How's your wife doing? Is she feeling better?" He said, "I don't know." "Well, I heard she was sick," I pressed. He said, "I don't know. She's not speaking to me. She's done nothing but grunt at me for three days. She's got a mad on." I was uncomfortable…I didn't even know how to respond. The first thought that went through my head was "What did you do?"

I understand being mad. I understand that sometimes it's better to turn away. Being a get-it-out-on-the-table kind of person, there are times I need to back off, because that sword of a tongue I have will cut somebody if I don't grab ahold of it. Wayne is a preacher; every argument has three or four points and a conclusion. I have to let him know, "You're pushing me too far. Something ugly is coming out…." So, I've learned that I need to back off when things get heated. But we need to be careful! If we're being hateful and just not speaking to them to be hateful because we're mad, that's not okay. That's not respectful.

So basically, being respectful is never say or do anything that lowers the way you see your husband or lowers the way anyone else sees your husband. I still have my moments; I'm human. But I'm so much better at it than I was before. I've learned that if I let those thoughts come into my head, if I start thinking belittling thoughts about him, there's trouble ahead. *"Man, if he would only… if he would only…."* I start feeling it. It starts making me look at him differently. Controlling those thoughts in the first place is so important. Be very careful of being respectful.

Another part of our role when we say "I do" is to become a lover. That's a huge part of our marriages. We're not talking about it in the church, and it's a real problem, even within Christian marriages. But we're going to talk about it in the third chapter that I write for you. Now, you can relax, because I'm not going to get detailed or anything. That would make me vomit. But we are going to talk about it.

When we say "I do," we also become a friend. Song of Solomon 5:16 says, "This is my beloved, and this is my friend." My husband is my best friend. I can't even imagine my life without Wayne. He is the one that I **want** to spend time with. There is nothing wrong with going to the movies with friends. There's nothing wrong with going to lunch with your girlfriends. But, when that is your preference over spending time with your husband, there's a problem and you need to fix it. Again, if you're thinking, *"Yeah, but he...,"* remember, we're not talking about him. We're talking about us: what we can do as wives and how can we make something better in our marriages by asking, "What can I do to make that better?"

Make sure you're working to build a friendship with your husband. It doesn't mean you have to do everything together. You both need healthy friendships. Remember when you were dating and he would say something like, "I'm going to just hang at home and watch football today"? Your response would be, "That sounds great; I'll be right over." But you really don't like football—you just want to spend time with him and show him that you were willing to try different things to build that friendship. Rekindle your friendship with your husband! Plan something he likes to do to do together! Or focus on the activities that you already enjoy together…just plan something.

Homemaker is the next aspect of our role as a wife. Now, back in my day, that meant that the wife was waiting at the front door in pearls and heels when her husband got home from work. Her house would be magazine-spotless and there would be a candlelit table with a perfect dinner on it. The children would be dressed in their Sunday best and sitting quietly on the couch. Do you see why the term *homemaker* was overwhelming for me? This is based in Titus 2:5, "Older women, teach the younger women to be the keeper of the home." After studying this passage—and no, I wasn't looking for a **loophole**—I found a deeper meaning. The phrase "keeper of the home" actually means "to guard the home" in the Greek. Our role as the wife is to guard the home. That means to set the tone in your home. Is your home a place of peace? Is your home a refuge for your family to come home to?

You want to make sure your husband is not looking for ways to keep away from home. If he is, we may have to make some changes. We need to make sure we're setting a tone in our homes that allows our husbands and our families to come home to a peaceful place. It doesn't mean you're the cook, the maid, and all of those things. But some of those may tie into it.

In my home I had to learn to keep house a little bit better than I probably would have otherwise, because I'm a little more laid back, and Wayne is a bit more…orderly. Wayne's mom used to iron sheets and that puts a lot of pressure on a person. For him to feel at peace in our home, I had to learn to keep things pretty orderly for him. That's tough with five kids! I also did daycare for 25 years in my home. So, we had to find a way to make sure that our home was a refuge for him to come home to. We also needed a regular routine of meals and bedtime for our home to be peaceful. But you have to set down with your husband and talk about what a peaceful home looks like for your family. What makes your home a refuge for your family?

I'm watching younger families work **together** better than families in my generation and those generations older than me and I **love** it!! Husbands are stepping in and helping more around the house. They are working better together as a team. Just keep in mind that it is still your role. Talk about it and make a plan together for your family.

Let me throw in a warning here. Be careful of comparing your home to someone else's. That's not fair to you or to them. We also need to be careful as older women of judging younger women on what **we think** their homes should look like. And yes, I've done that. But I have learned to step back and just encourage them to figure out what works in their home. Every home will be different. Find what works for your family and guard your home.

I'm not going to go into the Proverbs 31 woman, because all of the description of who she was is overwhelming. Some days I'm doing one or two of her characteristics pretty well; other days not so great. And just when I think I've nailed a couple of them, life changes and I have to start over. But I just keep striving.

I call the journey of marriage from stilettos to orthopedic shoes. That's our role as wives. We start out in the beginning of our marriage—and I don't care if you were 55 when you got married—we call it Stilettos because we think, *"Hot dog, I'm married. Things are good. I'm so in love! I love him so much!"* It's that part of marriage where it's just so fresh and wonderful. When we start out in the beginning, you ask, "Do you want Flip-flops?" "Yes, I'm Flip-flops. You want Hiking Boots?" "Yes, I'm Hiking Boots." It's the Stiletto phase where everything is new and exciting.

Then we started having babies, and it was into Running Shoes. I had to get tennis shoes to keep up with those kids. Having children affects your marriage. Remember, if you're in that stage in your marriage, your husband comes first. This is another problem area. In so many marriages, the wife totally becomes Mommy, forgets about being the wife, and when those babies are gone, she doesn't know how to be the wife anymore.

When the wife becomes Mommy and nothing else, the husband has no one. This is one way that Satan works on our godly husbands. We need to make sure that he understands that he still comes first. I know we can't say, "I've put the baby in the basement for the weekend, so it's just you and me!" That's not real. But remember him; let him know he comes first. He's more important. *"I've got to deal with the baby, but I know you're there. I'm coming back to you. Want to come sit with me while I feed the baby?"* That's a real stage of marriage. Don't push your husband to the curb during that stage. Have date nights! Make sure you figure out how to do this. It doesn't have to require spending a bunch of money. I have a friend that has a bunch of little ones and on date night they put the kids to bed early, like 6 and then have the evening to themselves. Babysit for each other as young parents. Older women reach out to these young families! Get to know them so that they have someone they trust with whom to leave their children.

Then I went into a phase of my marriage when I actually didn't know if I was Stilettos or Running Shoes or **what** I was. I was **really** struggling! I remember being a young woman, looking at older women in this stage, wondering, "What is wrong with those women?" I would hear them voice statements like this, *"I've got to find myself, I don't know who I am anymore."* And in my head, I'm thinking, *"You're right there. I don't get this."* Until I hit that phase. The last of my children had gone into school, and life was different for me. I still was doing daycare in my home, but my role was changing. Even if you do home schooling, your role changes. When those children who were so dependent on you move into a stage in which they have so much independence—you know that stage—it happened to me and I started thinking, *"Wait, who is Tami? Who am I? I have to find myself. I don't even know who I am anymore."* My role as Mommy had taken so much of my time, and now life had shifted. It was a real struggle! I always prided myself in being this strong, independent woman, and I suffered.

In fact, the first thing that I did was I started controlling the outer body. I know I'm not a big person. My teeny, bitty grandma blessed me with the frame I have. But I decided I was going to get in the best shape I'd ever been. I exercised, and I was very toned. One Sunday night at services I wore a skirt that was very modest, and a white eyelet frilly blouse, also very modest, and cowboy boots. I had three men tell me how nice I looked. Nothing inappropriate was said but it made me **very** uncomfortable.

It hit me what I had done. I had been so focused on the outer part of me that I'd let my heart go. That's real for a lot of women. So many women hit that stage, and I hear them talk about going to the gym. "Spent 22 hours at the gym this week." So many become body builders at this point because they've lost who they are. This is real! Now, I'm not saying that there's anything sinful with going to the gym. I want to make sure that you understand that I'm not spanking you if you're going to the gym. Just remain balanced. If you've gone through this, reach back and help somebody through it. Let them know they're not nuts, that they can get through it, and it's going to be okay. I had to learn to communicate to Wayne. I told him, "I don't know who I am anymore." He didn't get it. His advice was to get a hobby, which made me want to poke his eyes out of his head. But I had to communicate, saying, "Honey, I'm hurting, I'm struggling." Make sure you're talking in that weird part of life, that stage that so many call "midlife crisis." Pour yourself into the Word of God. Surround yourself with God's people.

Then I went back into High Heels. They weren't Stilettos; they were Pumps. It's the phase I'm in right now. My children are all married and living lives of their own. Oh, I still want to sit them in a corner sometimes and tell them, "You can get up when you remember how to behave." When I finally realized

I couldn't control them anymore, God settled His peace on me because I have turned them over to Him. Wayne and I can do things together, all kinds of things, and not worry about the kids being right there. It's a wonderful phase of life, and I love it! You might ask, "Oh, don't you hate the empty nest?" At first, it was a struggle for me. We are a loud family, so when those people were all gone, I was telling Wayne, "You've got to make some more noise, honey. It's quiet in here." We had to find ways to fill our home and make sure our marriage was strong. But it's a great phase of life.

As I look down the road—and it's not very far—I see the Orthopedic Shoe stage. My mom has always had issues with her feet, so she's always worn these nursing type shoes. Those shoes were **not** attractive in the '70s! As a teenager I always prayed, "Please, God, don't do that to me. Please, God, don't do that to me." Because I didn't want to wear those ugly nursing shoes.

Recently I was in an outlet mall in California, in a shoe store and there was this display on an endcap that described the shoes placed there as "Like Walking on a Cloud" or maybe it was "a pillow." I'm looking at these shoes, thinking, *"Okay, those aren't bad."* I actually thought they were pretty cute, so I tried them on. It was like heaven! It **was** like walking on pillows. So, the teenage girl that worked there came around the corner and I asked her, "Okay, you've got to be honest with me. Look me in the eyeball and tell me, are these old lady shoes?" And she said, "No...." You have to picture a teenager looking petrified that she's going to hurt an old lady's feelings but doesn't want to lie. "No, really," I told her, "really, I need to know—do these looks like old lady shoes? She said, "No, they're kinda cute. I said, "Well, it doesn't matter, they're comfortable and I'm going to buy these shoes today." I walked out of the store and I showed them to Wayne, who said, "You bought old lady shoes." Yes I did, and they are **so** comfortable! That's the Orthopedic Shoe stage. It's that stage of marriage where things are comfortable. It's where you are when you've worked through marriage. I'm not naive. That Orthopedic Shoe stage holds some different needs as well—health issues, money issues. It's that stage of life when you know that you have worked for, even fought for, your marriage.

That's what we want in our marriages. We want those marriages that stand strong. We're going to have struggles, and we're not always who we're supposed to be. We are just striving, and we won't quit. We make mistakes, but we get back up and we try again. Hang in there! I'm praying for couples that fight for their marriages. Couples that will look back and say, "Yes, it was hard, but it was **so** worth it!"

- Under the umbrella of respect, how can you lift your spouse up with your words?

- Make a "They're My Best Friend Because…." list.

- What changes are necessary for your home to be a better place of refuge?

- What phase of marriage are you in? How can you strengthen your marriage in this phase?

CHAPTER 4

FINDING THE "PERFECT FIT": MAKING IT WORK

Tami and I once drove from Denver to California by way of Las Vegas, Nevada. It's about 12 hours from Denver to Las Vegas. So, we made that our first day's drive and stopped in "Sin City" for the night, much to the shock of many friends and fellow church-goers. I will tell you, Sin City has the same sins as every other town. They just put marquee lights around it; that's the big difference. Nevertheless, we spent the night there, and kind of did the touristy thing of walking down the strip of Las Vegas to see all the casinos, the shopping areas, the lights and neon. As we were walking, I noticed that all of the ladies were carrying their shoes. I mean, they were wearing these nice dinner dresses, but carrying their shoes! I thought, *"Well, it must be some kind of an awareness walk, and people are being supportive of something."* In a little bit, I asked Tami about it. "Do you see all these ladies carrying their shoes?" Tami said, "Well, of course they are." Now I was really confused, because she knew something I didn't know. "What's up with that?" I asked. "Well, here's what happened," she said. "Earlier today, they had the perfect outfit for the dinner or the show, and they laid it out with the purse and the jewelry. They had all the accessories and picked out the perfect shoes. Then, they put them on, and they walked...and they walked...and they walked. They found out that, while those were the perfect shoes for how they looked with the outfit, they weren't the best for walking on the hot streets of Las Vegas. So now they have become simply an accessory to carry for the rest of the evening."

Sometimes it can be that way with our marriages. What we end up doing, if you will, is dragging our spouses through the rest of our lives because they have become uncomfortable or even worse, just throwing them or the marriage out.

Time to get really personal. Ladies, what's the deal with you and your shoes? The national average for American women is 20 pairs of shoes! Of those women, most only wear five or less on a regular basis. Here's the surprising statistic (at least to a man). Most women have at least one pair of shoes in their closet right now that have been worn only once or **never** at all. Why is that? If you only have two feet, why so many shoes? Here are some of the reasons I've been given these reason for why they buy shoes (A man's thought added):

> *They were cute! I saw them, and I just had to have them!* (Note: "Had to")
>
> *They completed the outfit. I have the dress, purse, jewelry…* (or I could get them).
>
> *They're what everyone is wearing* (Everybody??).
>
> *They were on sale!* (Just look at the long receipt to see what she "saved").
>
> *They are comfortable* (ugly as sin, but comfortable).
>
> *They stay the same size, even if I don't* (not going there).

What about you, guys? Why do we men buy shoes? Typically for only two reasons: The old ones wore out (or your wife threw them out) or functionality. We have dress shoes, work boots, golf shoes, running shoes, and cowboy boots (even if we don't have cows).

Considering all these reasons people give for making a shoe choice, don't you think it is likely that we—at least some of us—used the same reasoning to get our spouses in the first place? If he is cute or she is pretty, we bought on the basis of looks. Maybe we felt that they somehow completed the outfit. After all, it seems silly to have "his and her" towels if there's not a "his and her." Perhaps there's a functionality aspect. We think, "Well, I would like to have a companion for the rest of my life. I'll get a husband (or a wife)." Or, "I'm going to want to have a baby someday, and it's good to have a husband (or wife) before you have the baby." Some might have been thinking, "I want somebody to provide for me." Or maybe "I want somebody to cook and clean for me." I don't know what your version of functionality is.

Or maybe it was that everybody has one. I remember when a young girl came to me and said, "All my friends are getting married. I don't even have a boyfriend. I am going to be an old maid." I said, "You're 22. Relax. You've got a lot of time." We do that sometimes, though, don't we?

The difference is that we can't pick our spouses like we would pick a pair of shoes, and then when they don't work out well or fall out of fashion discard them to the corner of the closet and get another pair. At least we shouldn't. So how are we going to make our shoes fit? How are we going to find the fit that lasts for a long time?

There are times in life when it feels like our shoes don't fit just right. Sometimes, what seems in the beginning to have been the perfect fit ends up not being that way over time. Finding the perfect fit comes through breaking in those shoes and can come with some blisters and callouses, too. If we're not careful about finding our fit, "blisters" can develop and leave us calloused for years to come.

I want you to consider some principles that I believe that will help every marriage no matter what condition it's in to find its fit. If, right now, your marriage seems to be plagued with all kinds of blisters, these are some principles that will make the going better. Perhaps you are a couple of whom you would say, "You know what? I wouldn't just say we have blisters. Those blisters have become callouses; there's just not much feeling left there!" These principles will benefit you. If you would say, "I think we have found our fit," and as such, you're thinking, "I don't know that we need to work on it," I would suggest that these five principles will take your marriage to another level of comfort that you never even realized was possible.

In other words, these are principles that will help move your marriage from struggling, past surviving, all the way to thriving. They will ultimately help it become not only the blessing you want it to be, but the blessing God intended for it to be. Sometimes our problems come, and they're big. Sometimes we've got to work, and there's some giant hills to climb. Sometimes the difficulties are little things, but they can be just as aggravating. There's an old proverb that says, "It's the pebble in our sandal, not the incline of the hill, that makes the journey hard." So, what we want to do is find a kind of model that will help us in good times and in bad times.

HAVE A GOD-FIRST, GOD-CENTERED MARRIAGE

I am convinced that if there is any one principle essential for a thriving marriage, it is this: **put God first**. Now, for most people, they associate that with something like, "Well, we believe in God, we read the Bible, and we go to church. We follow Jesus and we're nice to people. She's a Christian; I'm a Christian. As such, we have a God-first marriage." I want to kind of go from that 30,000-foot view down to a 300-foot view and look a little closer at what it means to have a God-first marriage.

To see a God-first marriage, we must go all the way to the very beginning: Genesis 1 and 2, where God establishes marriage. Mankind may think it thought marriage up. The truth is that God is the one who established it. He created Adam, He created the perfect mate Eve, and He established the relationship that we call marriage—the relationship between a husband and a wife. A God-first marriage has to start with **God's design** as part of it.

We have a lot of discussion in our world today about so-called alternative lifestyles, and the argument often is boiled down to some bumper sticker statement like, "Well, the Bible says Adam and Eve, not Adam and Steve." It's really more important than that. It's more than just an argument over these same-sex attractions. It's really an understanding that, for marriage to be what marriage is supposed to be, it's going to have to be according to the design. In southern California there is a guy who tried to marry his horse. Now, you might like horses. You might love horses. But, let me just tell you right now, that relationship will never be everything that God intended a marriage to be on so many levels. It has to be according to God's design. And God's design is this: one man, one woman, for one lifetime. Now, I understand some things happen along the way, but that's the design, if you will, on the box. That's what this thing called marriage is supposed to look like.

But it goes beyond simply one man, one woman, for one lifetime. It also has to have **God's objective** in mind. Now, almost every man will understand this, because somewhere in his toolbox he has a butter knife. It's a butter knife that he took out of the silverware drawer, used as a screwdriver inside the washing machine, and ruined it. He couldn't return it to the drawer, so he put it into his toolbox. When you wives wonder, "How come I only have seven knives?," check your husband's tool box.

Now, a knife makes an okay screwdriver, but do you know what makes the best screwdriver? A screwdriver! It's what it's designed to do. Here's the thing, marriage can do a lot of things, especially in our world today; but ultimately God has an objective for marriage. God has a purpose for marriage. And a God-first marriage is not about what I want out of a marriage, or what my spouse wants out of a marriage. It's about what God wants out of our marriage. That comes back around; that's also good for you and that's also good for your spouse, because that's what God has in mind for you. A God-given objective is important.

As you think about that, remember that God is more concerned with our holiness than He is with our happiness. It's not that God doesn't want us to be happy. But God wants us to be happier than the version of happy with which we're often satisfied. God has something so much more in mind for our marriage. So, a marriage must set before itself the objectives that God has laid down rather than the objectives such as, "I just want a baby," "I want somebody to provide for me," "I want somebody to cook and clean for me," "I want a friend and companion." It is about looking at an objective that is so much higher than that.

Beyond that, a God-first marriage with that objective in mind allows God to be the one that directs the marriage. In other words, it needs to be **according to God's instruction**. It's how to build what's on the box, for the purpose of which the thing on the box is pictured on the box. Does that make sense? To the men it doesn't. We don't like instructions. We pride ourselves on being able to assemble a bicycle on Christmas Eve and still have parts left over. That's why we have garages. It's a place to store all the parts we have left over. When our wives come to the door, saying, "Now can I get the instructions?" We say, "Well, of course you can, but don't read them to me." It's similar to why men don't use maps. Why? *"We're not lost. We're just taking a different route this time."* But, for us to arrive at the destination God has set for our marriages, we're going to have to use the map—His Word—to get us there. Now, sometimes that map isn't going to make sense. Sometimes we're going to think, "I don't think that's the way to do it." But it is.

Tami and I were driving in Houston, Texas, and we were using the map app on her iPhone. It said to get off of the highway at the upcoming exit. I said, "That can't be. This is the highway we go on." I complied with the instruction anyway (see I can follow instructions!). We were hardly off the highway before Siri said, "Now, cross the street, get back on the entrance ramp, and merge onto the highway." I thought, *"See, I knew I was right. Siri doesn't know what she's talking about. I should have just stayed on the highway."* But, you know what? She was right. There was a toll bridge in between where I got off and where I got back on. She saved me $1.25 by having me get off and get back on. I love her, okay? I speak fondly of Siri. More about that relationship later. Here's the point. Sometimes God says about our marriages, "Get off at this exit." We think, *"That doesn't make any sense."* Or, "Get back on in this particular place," and we think, *"That doesn't make any sense."* But that's because we have our objective and our direction in mind, rather than God's objective and direction. A God-first marriage is going to be that which seeks God's help and God's guidance through regular study of His Word.

A God-first marriage is ultimately about **bringing glory to God**. There are people in our world today that have no idea why they're standing on this big blue marble spinning out in space. They're looking for answers at the edge of a bottle or the edge of a ledge. They don't have any idea what their purpose in life is. Here's your purpose. This is extra. No charge. You are here to glorify God. That's why He made us. God didn't sit in eternity and think, *"Oh, I am so lonely. You know what I should do? I should create some thick-headed, stubborn people to make Me feel loved."* God created us to glorify Him. He gave us what He gave us so we would live in such a way that it might ultimately bring glory to Him. He sent His Son to save us that He would be glorified for His mercy, love, and grace. It is impossible for us to have a life's purpose of glorifying God if we are sneaking a piece of the pie called "marriage" over here just for us. Our marriages have to be consistent with that purpose.

What does a God-first marriage look like? It begins by using God's design, setting before it God's objective, and listening carefully to God's instruction. Ultimately rather than asking, "What do I get out of it?" or "What does she get out of it?" or "What do we like/what do we want/what do we think?", the question becomes "Does this thing called marriage glorify God?" Only then does it become a God-first marriage. If your marriage is going to thrive, it's going to have to **put God first**.

LEARN TO SACRIFICE

Now, for most Christians/church-goers/Bible-readers, there are two predominant images of sacrifice. In the Old Testament, it is that picture of an animal split gut to gullet, thrown up on an altar, and consumed by fire or fumed to God. Not really the most romantic of imageries, right? Or we come to the New Testament, and there is a beautiful picture of Jesus dying on the cross, giving His life for all mankind. Again, though it's beautiful, it's not really the Hallmark card that we look for on Valentine's Day. But sacrifice is at the heart of a marriage that thrives. It is the kind of perspective that changes how a marriage looks day by day. We typically use the word *love* referring to the physical attraction that we have to somebody. *"I love him/her," "I love my mom,"* or *"I love a cheeseburger."* Each is a little different, but we still understand that each refers to emotion.

The kind of love we are to have for our spouses is completely different. It is a self-sacrificing love. It's defined this way: a choice action that seeks the well-being of another over oneself. That's the love that in a marriage is a lasting love, an enduring love, a building and strengthening love. On one hand, it is the easiest kind of love, because it doesn't require a relationship. It doesn't require a history together. It doesn't require circumstances that have been shared. It's not the result of something that has been done or something that will be received in return. In other words, it's possible for me to walk into any group of people, whether I know them or not, and say, "I love you." I seek your well-being over my own, even though we have no relationship whatsoever. That makes it an easy kind of love because it's just a choice to love.

It is also the most difficult kind of love, because we love those whom we like. We love those with whom we have a relationship, whether it's a friendship or a family relationship. We love those with whom we have experienced something together, or with whom we share something in common. Or perhaps they've done something for us, or we've done something for them, and as such we expect some kind of return. That's not the kind of love that's described. The kind of love to be exhibited in our marriages simply says, *"I choose the well-being of another over myself. I choose the well-being of my spouse and am willing to sacrifice for him (or her)."*

I once heard a story that I think illustrates this kind of love perfectly. Once a man walked into a church building. He was obviously homeless. His hair was a mess, he was dirty, and his clothes were in shambles. He didn't even have any shoes on his feet. He was walking from person to person panhandling for cash. Some of the men approached the man. They couldn't have him coming to panhandle because it made people uncomfortable. But at the same time, they had a genuine concern for him. They also wanted to find out what they could do to give some help in his current circumstance. As they were talking to him another guy walked up and handed the man a pair of shoes—someone recognized the man needed a pair of shoes, so he gave him a pair. What was so moving about it was that the man giving the shoes away was a man who had come just a few months earlier, asking the congregation if they could buy him some shoes because he didn't have any. He took those very shoes off his feet for the sake of the other man.

Now, I realize that's not a marriage, but the principle is the same. In other words, in my marriage, am I more concerned about the needs of my spouse than I am about myself? That becomes that kind of satisfying love which is not only a blessing to a marriage, but until you've truly experienced it, you don't realize that it's a blessing back to you. It's good for you. As they say, it's better to give rather than receive. Put your spouse first and learn to sacrifice.

IMITATE GODLY EXAMPLES

Let me explain what I mean by this. Find a couple who is living the way that God wants them to live in their marriage. Look for a couple whose life says, "We're pursuing a God-first marriage, and we're seeking to be the kind of couple that God wants us to be," and learn from them. Someone who you can talk with, confide in, seek counsel from. Find a couple you can use as a good example of how God's principles for marriage look in real-life and imitate. Now you may be thinking, *"Well, they're not going to understand what I'm going through; for them everything is perfect."* You'll be surprised. You'll find shortly after talking with them that they have had problems with addiction, with abuse, with unfaithfulness, with jobs, and the same kinds of things that you're facing. They have found their way through those things with God's help and can help you through them as well.

Here's the thing. We get God's instruction book out, and we start looking. What is our marriage supposed to look like? We read it, we read it, and we read it. Then we put it aside and we think, *"Yeah, but what does it look like in real life, day to day, when we encounter problems with a job, or problems with children, or problems with in-laws, or a problem with the plumbing? How does this thing look?"* That is where godly examples help. It's not about comparing and saying, "They're great and we're not." It's about working on it over time with their example as help.

I want to caution you, because sometimes what happens is that we become **impostors** not imitators. We pretend to be something we're not. Have you heard about a couple getting a divorce and thought, *"I can't believe it? They seemed so happy. I thought they were the model couple."* They may have been just acting like they were happy, but that was just on the surface. They weren't working to really be what they needed to be. One day, the facade falls down, and the marriage falls apart. Don't just pretend to be that kind of a couple, but really seek to be an imitator.

I also want to caution you about being an **impersonator**. When I was growing up there was a guy by the name of Rich Little. Rich Little did impressions of celebrities. One of his impressions was of John Wayne. He would put on a cowboy hat, walk with a swagger about him, and he'd say, "All right, pilgrim, circle the wagons," in that deep, gravely iconic voice. Everybody would say, "He's John Wayne!"

In 1969, I got to meet John Wayne when he was filming the original *True Grit* in Colorado. He wasn't really anything like what Rich Little had impersonated. He did wear a cowboy hat. He did have a notable swagger. I understand that came from wearing a girdle in the last years of his acting career (I know. It's hard to imagine, but supposedly true). And as any woman who has worn a girdle can tell you, that will give you a swagger. His voice most certainly was distinctive. What Rich Little really did was take two or three characteristics and exaggerated them. He wasn't trying to become John Wayne. He became, if you will, a caricature of what John Wayne was, using those familiar characteristics.

Sometimes what we do in imitating godly examples is to just become impersonators. We pick two or three things, and we embellish them. "They hold hands. We should hold hands. He has a nickname for her. I think we should. Don't you think so, Sweetie-Pie?" They do this; they do that. It's not about just **imitating** those things. It's about **becoming** the kind of people that they are.

Find those godly examples. Seek their counsel. Seek their advice. Seek their wisdom. Be open and honest in sharing with them. You will be so surprised about how they are able to share with you, explaining elements of their marriage about which you said, "So that's how it looks in real life."

FULFILL YOUR ROLE

There is hardly a marriage counseling session in which I have been involved that did not begin with one spouse wanting to fix the other spouse. Let me tell you a sad truth. I say sad because it's difficult to accept. There is only one person in a marriage you can fix, and that's you. You can ask, advise, encourage, even threaten, but you **can't** change another person.

Let me put it this way: your spouse's feet may stink, but so do yours. Sorry, they do. Ever met somebody that didn't know their feet stink? I remember once when my son came in from playing ball with some of his college buddies and kicked his shoes off in the family room. The smell was horrible. You know how in a cartoon green gas floats up from a witch's cauldron? I believe I saw that coming from his shoes. His young son shouted, through his hands that were covering his nose and mouth, "**Dad**, your choos 'tink!!!" And they did 'tink. Unbelieving, my son picked one of them up, buried his nose in it, and took a deep breath. "No, they don't." he reported. Oh, they did. He just wasn't very sensitive to his own odor.

Ladies, have you ever been to somebody's house, and it has **their** smell? It may not be a bad one. It might make you think, *"Oh, it smells like a potpourri factory exploded in here."* But, it's their smell. Or you think, *"I'm not sure, but I believe they had goat for dinner last night."* You might experience this and begin to worry. "I wonder if my house smells!" You go home, take a deep breath, and say, "Oh good, our house doesn't have a...." Let me interrupt you. Yes, it does. It smells like you and you just don't realize you have a smell. We all need to start to fix a problem in our marriages by smelling our own shoes.

Now, I understand that when problems arise in a marriage, the fault does not always lie equally with both spouses. For example, in matters of addiction, the problem may not have anything to do with one spouse, and it may have virtually everything to do with the other spouse. In a case of sexual unfaithfulness, it probably is not the fault of the one who didn't cheat. But the point is that the best place to begin in any such situation is to ask yourself, "Am I being the best me that I can be?"

I had a counseling session with a family. They were having more than marital problems. They were having family problems. This was a grown-up family. There were three generations all in one counseling session. I started off by saying, "Here's what I'd like to do. I'd like for each of you to state the problem in your family as you see it, and then I'd like you to tell me how you're contributing to the problem or how you're contributing to resolving the problem." So, I turned to the matriarch of the family. I said, "Grandma, state the problem as you see it." She stated her perspective. I said, "Okay, how are you contributing to the problem and/or how are you contributing to resolving the problem?" She began, "Well, my daughter…." I interrupted her. "Let me rephrase the question." I asked again, "How are **you** contributing to the problem or contributing to the solution?" Again, she says, "Well, my daughter…."

I thought, *"Okay, let's move over to Grandpa."* "Grandpa," I began, "how are you contributing to the problem, and how are you contributing to the solution?" He proceeded to tell me, "Well, my son…." Hoping to clarify, I asked the question again. Again, he began by saying, "My son…." We went all the way around the room with this kind of pattern. Finally, I was so frustrated I said, "Let me explain this one more time. I'm going to ask this question, and if anybody mentions anyone else in the family, you're going to see Jesus today" (I didn't really, but I sure wanted to). I promise this is what happened—I turned to Grandma and asked her, "How are you contributing to the problem, and how are you contributing to the solution?" She said, "My daughter…." Arghhhh!! You know what the problem was in their family? It was the attitude that says, *"The problems we are experiencing are everyone else's fault but mine."*

We need to be those who are learning to be the best "us" first, because that is really the only one person we can affect. You have a full-time job—being everything that you can be. Spend most of your time working on you. What does this approach produce in a marriage? Sometimes it produces nothing more than you being everything that you're supposed to be, because that's all you're going to give an account for one day. It may also have a value beyond that.

There's a young couple that Tami and I know well. He was not a member of the church; she was. He came with her and he was very pleasant. In fact, he and I became pretty good friends. One day he wasn't with her in church, but I didn't think much about it. Maybe he was sick. He wasn't there the next Sunday. Still not much concern, because he sometimes traveled with his job. On the third consecutive Sunday he wasn't there, I asked his wife where he had been. She replied, "It's really gotten bad at our house. Our marriage is falling apart. This religion thing has finally become a major issue. He doesn't agree with my beliefs and doesn't want me coming to church or bringing my daughters here. I think we may be close to a divorce over it." I asked if he would talk to me about it. She said, "No, he won't talk to anybody about it. It's bad, and I don't know what to do."

I said, "Well, I need to tell you that you've got two daughters that you're raising. You need to continue to raise those girls as a godly parent. You need to not lose your faith or lose your hope. You need to be what you're supposed to be. Be the loving and caring wife God wants you to be, and as time goes on, we'll see what we can do about him." I'll be honest. I said that, and it seemed to give her a degree of comfort. But, as I'm walking to the car, talking to Tami, telling her what's happened, I also said: "I'm not so sure that's going to make any difference, because ultimately they've got a problem that needs to be resolved. If he isn't willing to work to resolve it, I'm not sure her trying alone will fix it." Yes, I doubted my own counsel, even though I believed it to be the counsel from God's Word.

For quite some time, these kinds of a conversations went on with her. Sometimes I received from her a one-line email; sometimes she poured out her heart. Every time, not being able to give any another solution, I would say, "You've got to remain faithful. You've got to do what you're supposed to do. You've got to continue to be focused on being the godly person. You can't make him do it, but you can work to be that yourself." Every time I finished that email, I thought, *"It's been a long time, I have not had another answer to give her, and the problem isn't getting resolved."*

Then, I walked in one Sunday morning, and he was sitting there in the pew next to her. "Hey man," I said. "How are you? I've missed you." As he looked me right in the eye without blinking, he said, "We need to talk!" I thought to myself, *"Uh-oh, here we go."* We did talk, and we talked a little bit later that week. We talked a couple more times after that. At the end of that week, he came to an understanding of Scripture that resulted in him becoming obedient to Christ. He fixed his first relationship—the one with God—and it strengthened his relationship with his wife. They continued to be a faithful couple until his death a few years back.

I say all that not because her action changed him, but to make this point. What if she given up on being the best **her** that she could be? Had she just said, "You know what? I'm not going to do it anymore." What if she had become hostile in return, threatening or refusing to be the wife she knew she should be? I personally don't think he would have ever come to Jesus. Sometimes it's not the fault of their shoes at all. It's a problem with **our** feet. It's not the shoes that need breaking in; it's our feet that need some correction. We are well-served to work on ourselves before we start working on our spouses.

LEARN WHAT COMMITMENT IS

You remember the wedding ceremony, right? We all said it. "I promise," we said. "I promise to love, honor, cherish, in sickness, in health, for richer, for poorer, in good times and in bad, until death do us part." People make these promises. Then, someplace down the road, a couple comes in my office with a problem. Maybe it's a wife. She might say, "You know, my husband is addicted to pornography, and I know Jesus said in Matthew 5 that if a man looks at porn on the internet then he is lusting, which is the same as committing adultery. And since he has committed adultery, then I can divorce him and get another husband. Isn't that true?" That's not exactly what Jesus said, but I'll save that discussion for another time.

I always ask them the same question. "Is that what you're wanting? Are you looking for a way out of your marriage? Are you looking for a loophole to the promise that you made? Was the promise 'I promise…with the exclusion of if he ever gets addicted to pornography, or with the exclusion of this or the exclusion of that'? No. You made a promise, no matter what. It's a commitment." I don't want to seem insensitive and I am certainly not ok with using pornography, but a promise without condition is a promise without any condition. And a promise not kept is plain and simple a lie.

I kind of wish that we would change the whole "I do" element in our traditional vows. On that morning or that afternoon of the wedding, she's fixed herself up. He's taken a shower, combed his hair, and he's wearing a nice suit. Everybody has come because it's a great celebration. I mean, the day ends in cake! It's a great day. On that day, whoever is officiating looks at the bride and groom and asks, "Do you?" She says, "I do." He turns to him and asks, "Do you?" He says, "I do." I mean, of course they do **today**! But what about after the cake is gone? "I do" is an assent for the moment, however. It doesn't always carry with it the idea that says, "I will tomorrow and the next day and the next day and the next day." I kind of wish that we would change it to "I will." Because "I will" is not just an agreement to do it. It indicates that in the future, when I don't feel like it, I promise to **"will" myself** to do it. When I don't want to, or like to, or even think to…guess what? **I will.** My word is my word.

Again, I am not ignorant. I am not discounting those situations in which a marriage cannot continue. All I'm saying is that we are quick to run to an escape hatch in our marriage as soon as it doesn't go the way we want it to. *"I said in good times and bad times, but I didn't really expect it to be this bad,"* or *"In health and in sickness, but I never thought the sickness would be like this."* Some hear "for richer and poorer," but they didn't think that meant "dirt poor, we-ain't-got-nothing" times. So, they run to that escape hatch.

When you have an escape hatch in your mind, you'll only stay committed until you get to it. It's the escape hatch that says, "Well, we're going to try for a while." Or, "Okay, we'll give it a little time." Or "Until the children grow up." All we've done is just elongated the time until we race to the exit. Instead, we need to be those people who say, "You know what? I said, 'I will,' and I will."

There's a young man named Alex Sheen. Alex's father died, and his mother asked him to present the eulogy at the funeral. Sheen said, "I sat in my cubicle and I struggled, because my dad was nothing special." He said, "He was a good father and he was a good husband, but you know what? He hadn't invented anything. Hadn't discovered a cure for anything. He hadn't risen up the ladder of commerce or in academia; he didn't have a distinguished military career. He wasn't noted in the community for any one thing." He said, "I just realized my dad was an average guy, and I was saddened to think that as his son, the best I could come up with was that my dad was just an average guy."

"Then I realized that there was something unique about my dad that is just not as common as it used to be." He said, "My dad was a man of his word. If he told you that he would help you move on a Saturday morning at 9 o'clock, he was there at 8:45 with doughnuts in hand. If he told you he'd pick you up at the airport, you didn't have to call him the day before and say, 'Hey, Mr. Sheen, just needed to remind you, I'm needing picked up at the airport.'" Sheen said he was there faithfully. He said, "My dad was a man of his word. If he said it, he would do it."

Afterwards Sheen he thought, *"You know, I need to pass my father's legacy on."* He formed a Facebook group and a Facebook page in which he offered, to anyone who would send their name and address, to send ten business-card-sized cards that had printed on them, *"Because I said I would."* The idea was this: If you promised to do something for somebody, you wrote that on the card, and you gave that to them. When you fulfilled that task, they gave the card back to you as a reminder that you were working to become a person of your word.

Well, long story short, the whole thing blossomed to the point that Sheen is no longer a computer programmer, but he travels all over the world talking about being people of our word. And he talks about the fact that now those orders on any given day are more than 5,000 coming into his office, an office that now has not just a secretary, but an entire staff working toward this endeavor. It's a beautiful story to look up sometime and see how it has spread. Check it out at becauseisaidiwould.com.

I think that every single day, we need to give our spouses the card, literally or metaphorically, that says, "I will love you today because I said I would. I will do for you, even if it requires me to sacrifice, because I said I would. And if things are good, I will. If things are bad, I will. If we are rich, I will. If we are poor, I will. It doesn't matter, because I have made a commitment and I am a person of my word." If we want our marriages truly to survive, we need to quit looking for the loophole or the trapdoor, and realize, "I've got one pair of shoes, and I'm going to wear them for the long haul...."

That is how a marriage moves from surviving to thriving. Where it goes from being a millstone to being marked as a milestone in our life. That's what makes a great marriage, or at least gets us started on the right path. It doesn't fix every problem, but I believe no problem can be fixed until we start employing some of these principles to find our perfect fit.

HIS SHOES HER SHOES: SOLE MATES

CHAPTER 5

"HIKING IN HIGH HEELS": BEING A WIFE (FROM A HUSBAND)

The idea of *His Shoes, Her Shoes* came from the concept of each spouse considering their marriage from their spouses' perspective. Before we conducted our first seminar, I wanted to check if there was another seminar, book, or class called "His Shoes, Her Shoes" so we didn't infringe on someone else's stuff. When I did an internet search, the results brought up an image of a couple who had taken a picture of their feet to announce their engagement wearing red Converse Chuck Taylor All Stars. When I saw it, I told Tami, "I think we should do that. We should getting matching shoes to wear for our seminar."

We started looking around for matching Converse shoes. Much to my surprise they weren't the inexpensive athletic shoes I had remembered and worn in my youth. They were almost $60 a pair. However, we found one store offering orange ones at a substantial discount. I guess nobody liked orange. I loved them. Orange is my favorite color. I'm a Denver Broncos football fan and their primary color is orange **and** they're more than half off. I **love** orange. I don't know if you know this, but when it comes to size, Converse All-Stars don't really have men's shoes and women's shoes. They just have the men's/women's size marked on the end of the box. But we needed to find orange ones. Tami went off to the women's department to try to find a pair for her, and I went off to the men's department to find a pair for me. About the time I said, "I found a pair!" she also said, "Me, too!" We walked up to the cash register, and each set our shoe box up on the counter next to the cash register. Then, I saw something on the end of the box that was unsettling. Tami and I wore the exact same size shoe. It turns out that Tami and I could wear each other's shoes, but we don't. Her taste is different than mine and I don't have the legs for high heels. Have you ever really considered high heel shoes? Apart from the grief you would take from the guys for wearing them, do you realize how impractical they are? How about climbing a ladder or into a pick-up truck in high heels? I can't imagine standing in them all day or crossing a gravel parking lot or a really wet yard of grass. Imagine a mountain hike in high heels. I mean they aren't even shaped like a human foot, unless your middle toe is the longest. In spite of that, women wear them and seem to navigate just fine in them. I would find them uncomfortable, inconvenient, and constraining. I want you to think a little more about what it's like to wear your wife's shoes—not the high heels—but the shoes of responsibility that God has given her as a wife. We've already seen that husbands have an enormous responsibility. It's not easy to wear those big shoes. Well, God has given the wife a pair of very uncomfortable and constraining shoes that are equally difficult to wear. They are the shoes of submission. They're a pair of shoes that I don't think most men would want to wear.

We may think that we have the tough job as the provider and the protector. We have the 40-, the 50-, the 60-hour workweek, all the while carrying the family on our shoulders, and all our wives have to do is to parade around in the high heel shoes of what we consider to be weakness, to be passive, to just be a follower in submissiveness. Even though it may be difficult to be the man in the family, I don't think I could do what it takes to be the God-fearing, submissive wife in the relationship. It's a pair of shoes that many in our world today find disgraceful, when in fact they are some of the most beautiful shoes one could wear. I want us to have a better appreciation. I want you to understand what it's like to be a godly wife who seeks to live in those kinds of shoes.

As we begin, let's turn our attention to a couple of passages of Scripture. I work hard on not sound too much like a preacher who just throws Scripture out at the beginning of every thought, but I believe that the principles we are looking at here are all, ultimately, God-based.

Genesis 3: Here's the scene. Adam and Eve had eaten the forbidden fruit. God condemned the serpent, the devil in the flesh, for what he had done in deceiving them (vs. 14-15). God curses the ground; it would no longer readily give up its crops. He looked at Adam and told him that by the "sweat of his face" he would work for food (vs. 17-19).

In the middle of all of that, in verse 16 God turns to Eve, and says, "I will greatly multiply your pain in childbirth; in pain you shall bring forth children, yet your desire shall be for your husband, and he shall rule over you." God established this. The husband was given headship and his wife would submit to that rule. Although the sin of Adam and Eve did not pass on to every other man and woman, the consequence of that sin did; the husband will rule and his wife is to be in submission. Not a very popular position, but a true one.

The principle is reinstated in the New Testament. In 1 Peter 3, the apostle Peter reminds wives, "Be submissive to your own husbands." He illustrates that this is even true of a wife whose husband isn't submissive to God (vs. 1-4), who had probably heard the truth and rejected it. Peter instructs that the wife was to continue, even in that situation, to be submissive to her husband. So, it's not just a being submissive to a godly husband, but simply being submissive to your husband as a submission to God's design.

The apostle Paul continues the teaching, in Ephesians 5:22, "Wives, **be subject** to your own husbands" (emp. added). He further instructs when he write to a local preacher named Titus, telling him to have the older women teach the younger women to be "subject to their own husbands, that the word of God may not be dishonored" (Titus 2:3-5). Agree with it or not, it's pretty hard to get around such clear instruction from God.

The subject of submission is not celebrated in today's world. In fact, the world has given submission its own definition. It is not desirable and certainly not pursued. It's seen as weakness, inferiority, and dishonorable. It's considered by some as the result of a controlling or oppressive force. Many, when they think about submission, think about women because of traditional cultural norms and its association with the role of a wife in a marriage. All of these are interesting perspectives considering that the word we find in the New Testament translated as "submission" is not used only of women and was—in the first century—often used in a military context. It's defined as, "literally, to yield under, to arrange troop divisions in a military fashion under the command of a leader." In non-military use, "a voluntary attitude of giving in, cooperating, assuming responsibility, and carrying a burden." It communicated the idea of the organizational structure of a military campaign which ensured or at least worked towards the success of that campaign.

Now, I am not a military guy. I was not in the military. My father wasn't, either. I know some who were. So, if you're a military guy, I want you to excuse the following illustration. I say that because I always have somebody who speaks up about my understanding of how the military is or works. I said something at one of our seminars about a Marine drill sergeant. One guy, who was a Marine, walked up to me like some of them like to do, with this *"What is your major malfunction?"* look on his face, and said, "You know, drill instructors in the Marines aren't all sergeants." I said, smiling, "Well, this this one was." Relax, I'm grateful and have high regard for those who serve in our armed forces. Even the little, self-appointed generals.

Here's the way I understand it. There are generals and there are foot soldiers. The organizational structure demands that we can't have generals without foot soldiers. With only generals, they can plan a strategy (deciding what the campaign should be and how the enemy should be approached), but there is no one to execute those plans! The battle is lost even before it has begun. On the other hand, if we have nothing but foot soldiers (those who have been armed well, but have been given no direction, instructions, or strategy) for a time they may be successful in hand-to-hand combat, but the battle really is doomed to failure because they have no leadership. It takes both to achieve the desired result—victory. God has done the same thing within the marriage relationship. He established a chain of command to allow the family to function at its peak. It's not about who is superior. God has organized it in such a way that it works for the well-being of the family and to His glory.

It is essential that the husband take his leadership role. A major reason why families are failing, both in and out of the church, is because men are not being the men they are supposed to be. They are not taking their leadership role. Certainly, feminism is on the rise, promoting women who want to be men. But there are also women who are having to be men because men aren't being men. Somebody's got to drive the car. God has established that the man is the one to be leading the family and not the wife. At the same time, as valuable as the leadership role is, equally of value is role of submissiveness. It is an essential element! Without that role, the marriage is equally at risk of failing.

I understand that, in the arrangement of a helicopter rotor, there is one piece of that mechanism that is called "the Jesus pin" or "the Jesus nut." It's called that because, if it fails, the next person you're going to see is Jesus (or at least you'll be praying to Him). It holds everything together. Each part of the mechanism is independently valuable, each are dependent on the other parts, and it is all held together by this retaining nut. It's like that in God's design for our families. He says, "I have a plan for families. A plan to help it succeed. Each of you are an invaluable part of the plan, and it all goes perfectly together—and in my plan Jesus Christ is what ties that altogether. When you have that mechanism in place, victory is ahead."

I don't know if any of you have had any trouble starting your car in the morning? I remember when I lived in Colorado, we would have some really cold mornings. Occasionally, when I would go out really early on a cold morning to try to start the car, it would verbally tell me that it was not going to start. It would say, "Huh-uh, huh-uh, huh-uh, huh-uh," and then I would hear the dreaded *click, click, click, click*. I would storm back into the house saying, "I'm getting a car that'll start! I'm an important guy with important things to do, important work, and I can't be held back by a car that won't start!" The most important thing about a car is that it goes. A car is supposed to go!

But, at the same time, we've also learned that a functional car is supposed to stop. This is equally important. When my kids were all still at home, our family station wagon was in the repair shop and a friend lent me his 15-passenger van for the week. It was an old blue church van. That week we were on our way to church. We pulled into the church parking lot, and I applied the brakes because two clueless old women, bless their hearts, stepped right out in front of the van. (You know the "bless your heart rule," right? You can say anything about anyone as long as you end it with "bless your heart"). When they bolted out in front of me, I simply applied the brake and it went all the way to the floor. **No brakes**! I began to do what I believe is instinctually put in the mind of every man by God: Pump the brakes to get enough hydraulic fluid up to get this thing stopped! I think if a truck goes off a cliff, a man will be pumping the brakes all the way down, thinking eventually it's going to slow it down. The van stopped, and—I may have enhanced it just a little bit in my memory—one of the old women turned just enough for her nose to take the top layer of dust off the grill of the van. The kids in the back were screaming and had dug their hands into the seats. I had bent the steering wheel over, with beads of sweat running off of my face. The ladies didn't even look up and acknowledge me stopping. They just turned and kept walking. It turned out that the master cylinder was failing. It was then that I realized that a car which wouldn't stop isn't of any value, either. A car is supposed to stop too!

Now, I don't know in your marriage relationship if your wife is the starter or if she's the stopper. Perhaps she's the one who gets things going and you're the one who has to hold her back, or perhaps you're the one that's impulsive and out there, and she's the one putting the reins on, saying, "Let's think about this." But I do know this, that God has intended an organizational structure for your family in which a wife takes a role that is just as important as yours.

Submissiveness in general, as a quality of character, has fallen on hard times in our "You're not the boss of me" society. Neither men nor women really like the idea of being the submissive one. We like our own ideas. We like our own perspective. We like our own interests. It is really hard for us to turn our lives over to somebody else. Submissiveness really is an admirable characteristic. Those that view submissiveness as being a sign of weakness don't understand submissiveness. It is not a sign that someone has the inability to conquer and therefore they surrender. Some picture submissiveness as just giving in. Let's say that I decided to be a cage fighter. You know, one of those guys who goes face to face and fist to fist with another fighter in a fenced in octagon. For my first fight I draw a guy who is far better than I am. He is more muscular, has more strength, and is more experienced than I am. I waltz into the ring and immediately yell, "I submit!" I knew that there was no way I could win, so I just quit. In those fights they also have "submission" holds, but really by that point, you don't actually submit, you're beaten. You surrender because you don't want your arm pulled completely out of the socket. That's not what real submission is. Now imagine the same scenario, but instead of me submitting to a superior opponent, he submits to me. It could happen. He was clearly able to control the outcome but chose to surrender his will for mine. The submission of a wife is like that. It's a choice. She isn't saying, "I'm weaker" or "My husband is better." She is saying, "I may very well be smarter, I may be stronger, I may be better equipped…and I know I'm prettier—but I choose to step back to the role that God has given me." Her submission means "I could take the lead, but I won't." It is a volunteered submission to us and ultimately to God.

The view that we are the superhero of the family and that our wives are our sidekicks—the "Robin" to our "Batman"—is a misunderstanding of their role (and our ability). We are not the boss or master and she definitely is not our employee or slave. Submission doesn't mean lesser. We understand that from the person of Jesus. Paul describes Him this way, "Although He existed in the form of God, He did not regard equality with God a thing to be grasped, but He emptied Himself…He humbled Himself by becoming obedient to the point of death" (Philippians 2:6-8). Jesus humbled Himself. He submitted to the will of the Father for the sake of all of mankind. What all did He surrender when He submitted? I'm not sure I completely understand all of that. He is the Creator of the universe who depends on and answers to no one but became a baby who was dependent on parents to feed Him, change Him, and take care of Him. He is the all-knowing One, who for a time submitted, having to learn to talk, walk, etc. I don't even pretend to fully comprehend all of that. The best analogy I've heard to explain this section is this. Jesus is like a king over a kingdom who decides He wants to know what it is like to live amongst the common people. He takes off His crown, He takes off His robe, He lays down His scepter, and He puts on the rags of the world. He walks amongst the people. He looks like one of the commoners, but He is still the king. He is not lesser because He does this. The same is true of Jesus. Just because He took a place of submission, He was God, He is God, and will always be God. He was never less than the Father to whom He submitted.

That truth is verified by the word *existed* in verse 6. Our English translation chooses to translate it in the past tense, as if it's something that He was. Because that's good English grammar. But the word in the original language means "existing." That is, He always has existed as God, and always will exist as God, and has never not existed as God. Even when He took a role of submission, He **was** God and equal to Him. He never was "not God," therefore He can't, by definition, be a lesser. He **humbled** Himself. It's not the word *submission*, but it is akin to it. He made a choice to submit for a time—for you and me. That's what a wife does when she chooses self-emptying or submissiveness.

In the beginning when God created man and woman, He said, "Let Us create man in Our image, and let them have dominion over the world." The word *man* here is not gender specific. It's isn't confined to males only. It's like when we refer to mankind, meaning all of them, male and female. They were both created in God's image and both given dominion over the world. God made them equal. And it doesn't take a scholar who understands the original language to know that sometimes our wives are better at some things than we are. But, they surrender the control of those things! It doesn't mean that they don't contribute. It doesn't mean that we shouldn't default to their suggestions, ideas, or wisdom. It doesn't mean that they're not active. A submissive wife realizes what her role is. That doesn't mean she is of less value. In fact, it means she is even more valuable.

You know how a lot of girls are big into diaries. They love their diaries and they write in them. They write down everything they are thinking, everything they are feeling, and all their hopes and dreams. It's written in scrolly letters and dotted with flowers. Pink and purple ink fills the pages. It's the unfolding story of her life. On our wedding days, our brides gave the diary of their lives over to, of all people, you and me—the husbands. We hen scratch through it with whatever pen that we can find, and we forget some days to write in it, and we absolutely don't add flowers. The story of a wife's life—something in which she has and full control of—one day changes, and she allows her husband charge of it. That's not easy!

I don't know about you, but I don't like anybody to be in control of me. For example, I don't like to let Tami drive. When we would drive from Denver to Oklahoma City to visit our kids, it was a simple drive with just a single turn. The route runs straight east on I-70, hang a right at Salina, then take I-135 into Oklahoma City. Most of the trip is through Kansas. Kansas is full of very nice folks, but it is not the most exciting scenery after the 12th or 20th time through it, especially at the end of a day. It's warm in the car, and everyone is thinking, *Will we ever get home?* It's a 2-lane highway each way and sometimes it's a challenge not to take both of them. Tami is attentive, and has occasionally said, "You're getting sleepy, aren't you?" But, because I don't want her to drive, I'll say, "No, I'm fine." One day I said, "Fine." I pulled over. The wind was blowing about a hundred miles an hour. I climbed out of the car and she climbed over into the driver's seat. As soon as she put the car into drive and pulled into traffic, I was wide awake. I told her to pull back to the side of the road and I'd take it from there. Tami is an excellent driver. That's not why I don't want her driving. I like to do the driving, of the car and my life. In submissiveness our wives slide out of their driver's seats, take the passenger place, and give us the wheel, trusting us to steer their lives safely (but they may have a thing or two to say about our driving).

A wife turns control of her life over to her husband. Often in a wedding sermon I describe it this way. To the husband, I say, "The wife has paid you one of the greatest compliments that she could. She is going to surrender her name for you. She's going to take on your name." I like my name. I've always liked my name. I like something that says "Roberts." I could see a truck which said, "Roberts Trash Company," and I'd think, *"That's a good-looking truck!"* because it says "Roberts" on it. When I got married, my wife changed her driver's license and her Social Security card, and she's now Tami Roberts, not Tami Davison. I'm not sure I would like it if I had to do that. I like my name. I don't even want to be a hyphen. I'm going to be "Roberts." Ultimately, it's not about the name. It's about who leads. It's about submission. I don't want to give up my name because I don't want to give up control. But a wife gives up her name and the control of her life? She puts it in the hands of her husband to accomplish what needs to be accomplished for her and for their family.

When we were going to get married, Tami's parents offered us some money and said, "This is for your wedding. You may have a small wedding and keep the difference in cash, or you may have a big wedding and spend it all. That's up to you." I said, "Let's see the Justice of the Peace for $22, so we'll take the rest of it in cash! Thank you." Settle down, ladies; we had a nice wedding at her parents' home. She had a wedding dress, there was a wedding cake, and there was music. We had a nice little ceremony, but we got the rest of the money to spend. That was what we had in the bank to start.

A few weeks later, Tami came to me and told me she had a confession to make. She said, "I have been holding this in my wallet since the day we got married." It was a hundred-dollar bill. She said, "When I got my last paycheck, I took $75, folded it up and put it in my wallet, because I didn't know if you could provide for me and my son." Tami and I had a short courtship. Our first date was the end of February and we got married the end of June. We didn't know each other very well. She said to me, "I didn't know how good of a provider you would be. I was nervous about it." All I could think of was, *"We could have had cable."* She tried her best to say, "I'm going to surrender to somebody for my spiritual well-being, provision, and protection." But that isn't easy.

It isn't easy to let go and let someone else take control. Genesis 3:16 includes a little phrase that often gets overlooked. The original language kind of stumbles into English. God says to Eve, "But your desire shall be for your husband." Now, it might be that we simply think, *"Well, there's the punishment. You'll be in love with your husband, and that's punishment enough."* But it actually means she will want to be the leader of her own life. She will want to be in control of it. It is the way she was created. It won't come naturally. It will be a daily challenge for her to be submissive. You might be thinking, *"Well, it should be easy for my wife to be submissive to me. I am a loving, understanding, smart, sensitive, articulate man. It should be a breeze!"* Think again. It's hard.

Think of it this way—how about your own submission to God? God is perfect in every respect and has nothing but our best interest in mind. God has extended us favor when we have been the most rebellious. God is, simply put, perfect. And yet how challenging is your struggle to be submissive to Him? I don't know about you, but this is a daily struggle for me in one way or the other. And God is perfect. It's just not easy to let someone else take over.

Here's something else to consider. A wife's submission is needed for her husband to be all that God has called him to be. You cannot do it without her. You are incomplete without her. When God created the world, He described it as "very good." It means perfect. Not just without flaw, but perfectly designed to all work together. Then God creates Adam and says, "It is not good" (Genesis 2:18). Adam was alone and incomplete, so God created for him a wife, Eve. Her role is described as "a helper" or a "help-meet." Here's another one of those words that does not translate super well out of the original language. The full meaning can get lost in the translation. It might sound like she is just a hired hand (who doesn't get paid). For the best definition I defer to the ultimate authority on all things woman related—my wife. I took a peek at her seminar notes one day. I wanted to see what she planned to say about this idea of a help-meet. I wasn't sure that she wasn't just going to remind the ladies that there were more of them than there were of us on the earth and they could rule the planet if they wanted to. Turns out that was not her plan. Here is what she tells wives in regards to their role in marriage: their job is to be the gel insert for their husbands. Initially I thought, "Huh?!!! The gel insert?" That's not very flattering. That was until I wore those orange Converse athletic shoes we had bought.

The Converse Chuck Taylor All-Star shoes may be fashionable, and they may be, as some call them "hipster," but let me tell you right now, they are without a doubt the worst shoes in the entire world (at least for this old guy). There is no arch support inside! There is only a thin piece of formed rubber on the bottom. One of the first times I ever wore those for a seminar, I had to stand on a hard floor for the duration of the seminar. The next day I could hardly get out of the bed because my back hurt so bad. I then had to go to the old man section at Wal-Mart. It's where you find the knee and elbow braces, the corn and bunion pads, and the shoe inserts. I bought the cheapo ones, because I'm not going to buy the expensive, old, old man inserts. They were life changing. I could stand up in these terrible shoes and try to look fashionable while also being able to walk the next day without needing assistance. All I needed was the support help to do what I needed to do. That's what a wife does. She lifts us up as we fulfill our roles. That's her role. She helps to make our walk more comfortable. Our wives are not just a fashionable accessory; they are a valuable asset.

A wife's submission is all about love. A love for God, for her husband, and for her family. It's about sacrifice. It's all about giving up for the well-being of someone else. When our kids were little, somebody always needed a pair of shoes. It felt we'd buy a new pair of shoes on a Saturday; the kids wore them on Sunday and then the next Sunday they'd be all worn out or too small. I'd say, "Where are their new shoes?" And she would say, "These are the new shoes." But every once in a while, between shoe sizes, I'd suggest that Tami get a new pair of shoes for herself. She typically declined, citing that the kids needed new shirts, or they needed some jeans, or they needed socks, or we needed some more groceries. I'd say, "Why don't you get a new dress?" But, again, she would tell me the kids needed shoes, or we needed something else more than her new shoes. Then when my last kid moved out, and Tami went shoe-crazy. We went to a store and she had two boxes of shoes under each arm, a pair of sandals in her teeth, and was headed to the cash register. I said, "I didn't think you liked shoes! You never bought shoes when our kids were little." She said, "I've always loved shoes, but there was always someone else that needed something else more than I needed shoes." That's a snapshot of what submissiveness is. It isn't that she didn't need shoes. It isn't that she didn't want shoes. It's not even that we couldn't necessarily afford the shoes. But to do that would have cost the family something. It was her sacrificial spirit that says, "I will surrender my needs for your needs, what I want for what you want. I will seek the well-being of my family over my own."

It is a prized possession, this characteristic of submission. And the real beauty of it: she does it by choice. Because true submission is not just going along with something. It doesn't say, "Fine, we'll do it your way." Submission means a wife being fully supportive of her husband, not just "going along" with him.

It might be better understood in a corporate setting. Picture a big boardroom in which the board is meeting. There's some discussion or debate about a particular subject, a particular issue for the direction of the company. Let's just say that there are ten guys around the table. And one of them disagrees with the direction in question. He makes his case. He maybe even vocalizes his case very adamantly, even arguing his case. But finally, a vote is taken, and nine of the ten decide that it is the direction they should go. True submission, in a corporate setting that produces a great corporate growth model, is when that individual says, "I don't agree with it, but I won't just go along with it. I'll be fully supportive of it. I'm going to be on the front lines doing whatever I can do to see that it succeeds."

Whether it's in a corporate setting, a church-leadership setting, or in the marriage setting, it is a beautiful thing when one takes the route of submissiveness to the leadership of the others for the well-being of the whole. Our wives are constantly doing this!

Now, I know what husbands often think. *"Well, yeah, but I'm providing, right? I'm the provider for the family. I work 50, 60 hours a week so that my wife can have a nice home."* All she has to do is to decorate it and keep it clean.

"I gave her wonderful children" whom she has to care for and to raise when you're not there and to teach and to nurse back to health and to discipline in your absence.

"I'm going to give her nice things like clothes, because I'm a giving guy." All she has to do is see that they're laundered and mended and folded and put away. And when they get all dirty, she does it all over again.

"I'm going to fill the cabinets with food." All she has to do is to make nice, healthy, economical meals for the whole family; cook it, then clean up the dishes, and do it all again at the next meal.

"But I know she works hard, so I'm going to take her on vacation." All she has to do is see that the kids are packed and everything's ready to go. She can make sure there are some little snacks for the road. Then, when the family

gets back and has dirty clothes and dirty dogs and everything else, she'll take care of it because you've got to get back to work. All she needs is to sit there in submissiveness. She doesn't have to do much of anything. Here is her "not much of anything." Your wife wears high heels, work boots, combat boots, and nurse's shoes. She's a wife, a mother, a teacher, and a cook. She's the maid, she's a lover, she's a friend, a companion, and so much more. And she does it all in the little pointy, tight shoes called "submissiveness." When I start looking at her role from her shoes, let me tell you right now, I like those big, old, clunky shoes that I have to walk around wearing. I don't think that I would like to wear the shoes that Tami wears.

These are the beautiful shoes of a submissive wife. Submissiveness is a beautiful thing. It's not just a sign of a good character; it is a sign of godly character, which was personified in the person of Jesus Christ Himself. Submission is not easy. Anytime you think it is, all you have to do is remember your own submissiveness to Jesus Christ. Submission is a demonstration of love for another, but it is also an indicator of somebody who loves God and is submitting, not just to you, but to God as well.

It may be hard for us men to accept that when God looked at us, He said, "It's not good." But He did. Our wives have been given to perfect us, to make us fully functional. This does not mean a single guy cannot be beneficial to the kingdom and cannot be pleasing before God. But husbands have been given a special measure of blessing in our wives, who were given to help us do what God has called us to do.

I always say that submission should be greatly admired like a beautiful pair of shoes. But that doesn't mean much to guys. Think of your wife's submission with whatever picture works best. If you're a golfer, it's more beautiful than the green fairways of Augusta. If you're a fisherman, it's more beautiful than then clear, cool water of a Rocky Mountain stream and that 18" rainbow trout who's looking for the lure you just cast. If you are a hunter, it's more beautiful than that big old buck a few hundred yards away that turns broadside and looks at you as if to say, "I dare you. Shoot!" Her submissiveness is as beautiful as anything you can imagine. The next time you see a wrinkle or a gray hair or an extra pound here or there, just look straight down at those feet wearing the very constraining and uncomfortable shoes of submissiveness. Beautiful!

HIS SHOES HER SHOES: SOLE MATES

CHAPTER 6

THESE SHOES ARE TOO BIG: BEING A HUSBAND (FROM A WIFE)

This is my favorite lesson that I get to share with wives, in which we look at the husband's role in marriage from the husband's viewpoint. This is the whole "His Shoes, Her Shoes" perspective. When we decided to do our seminar, Wayne and I sat down and talked about our perspectives—how I see marriage, and how he saw his role in marriage. I also have asked men from different age groups how they see their role and how they feel about various aspects of marriage. I'll be sharing some quotes from them as I go through this lesson.

Keep in mind as I do this, though, that our job is not to change our husbands. We can only make adjustments to ourselves. I pray that, as I share, you're not making a checklist for your spouse. That's not my intention. Ladies, I know that some of our men aren't being the godly men that God has asked them to be. Sometimes we develop this preconceived picture in our heads of what our husbands should be. Maybe we compare them to our dads or to other godly men we know. That isn't fair! We **must** wipe our preconceived thinking out of our minds. I learned this very quickly in my marriage. I expected Wayne to act like my dad. Wayne would even tell me, "I'm not your dad." I felt like when he wasn't acting like my dad that his behavior was wrong. Well, I mentioned that my dad is this gentle, quiet man, and Wayne is the polar opposite of that. And I **love** that about him! When I let go of the thinking that he should behave like my father, my marriage improved because I saw Wayne differently.

Please keep in mind that the way your husband was raised will play into what kind of husband he is. If he wasn't raised in a Christian home, he doesn't know what a godly husband looks like. Even if he was, he isn't his dad and he's not married to his mom. So be very careful about putting expectations on your husband. Your expectations are just that—your expectations. It may be time for you to quit focusing on your expectations for him and look at God's expectations for you. I'm just sayin'.

The reason I am sharing this lesson is because we want to be able to lift our husbands up and to have a better understanding of their role in marriage. To wrap our hearts and minds around what that looks like and feels like for them.

Wayne started out with this description. "When I was a boy, I would put my small feet into my father's shoes and try to walk around in them. It wasn't easy! However," he said, "it wasn't until I was married that I understood that it took more than bigger feet to fill a husband's shoes." He said that once he became married, it was overwhelming for him, because he saw that the role involved so much more than just being a grown-up. It was much more complicated than that.

I want us to start by taking you back to your wedding day. We have the groom all dressed up in whatever you told him to wear, down to those shiny rented dress shoes. Usually the groom and his groomsmen and family are sequestered away somewhere waiting for their cue to make their entrance.

I have four sons and a daughter. My family is a loud, obnoxious, goofy bunch of people. Every one of us think that we are the funniest person on the planet. At the weddings of my sons, we would be off in the fellowship room or wherever we were gathered, cutting up and waiting for the moment when the parents were to go out to be seated and the groom is called to the front of the auditorium. We'd be laughing hard and just being silly. Then a person would come in or we'd hear that musical note, and I would look at my son and watch as his blood would drain from his body and pool on the floor. Reality would kick in. The whole demeanor in the room would change at that point. My eyes would get all misty and I would wander down the aisle. The groom then would step out, and we could see him standing there in his shiny rented dress shoes.

Let me challenge you—watch the groom at a wedding. When the doors swing open, everyone turns back to see the bride as she comes down the aisle. Watch the groom's face first. I get goose bumps just thinking about it. Because even those big, macho, burly men will well up with tears when they see their woman come to the door. Here she comes, and it's like everything is pretend. *"This is the moment I've waited on. I love her so much. She's so beautiful!"*

They go through the wedding ceremony—not remembering a word they say, by the way; when young people are planning their ceremony, they think, *"I have to make sure everything is perfect."* But I tell them, "No one knows but you and you will be so focused on each other you won't remember a thing." The bride comes down the aisle and it's this whole fairy tale kind of situation. Everything feels kind of pretend. The reception begins, time to meet all of the strangers and that also feels pretend. Even the wedding night and if you're lucky enough to have a honeymoon, it is all kind of a blur, very make believe.

Wayne and I got married on a Friday night in Broken Arrow, Oklahoma. I got married in my parents' home with immediate family (I told you—I was cheap). I had a dress, I had a cake, and I had flowers, the whole bit—it was just simplified. I loved my wedding! I love how we did it; it was so personal. We got married Friday night, spent Friday night in the Williams Plaza Hotel in downtown Tulsa, and Saturday got into a Ryder truck with our meager belongings and headed for Denver. We spent Saturday night in Wichita, went to church in Salina, and continued on into Denver that evening. We spent that first week of our marriage in the home of Wayne's parents as we looked at apartments. It all seemed pretend! Like we were "playing house." Wayne's mom picked our first apartment, our first home. It was perfect! We moved in and our life began.

Okay, I need to add a part of our story here just so that you have a better picture of Wayne's role. I mentioned that I have a rebellious spirit that I struggle with. Well, I was pregnant before Wayne and I got married. In fact, I was pregnant when he first noticed me. I was pretty noticeable…I was **huge**! Pregnancy is what woke me up and made me get my life in order. We started dating when my son was 2 months old and 6 months old when we got married. Our plan was to live in Oklahoma and both of us work. Well, Wayne is a Colorado boy and asked me if I would be willing to move to Denver. I told him that if he could find a job making what we both made, where I could stay home with the baby, then I would. So, he did; he got that job. That's how we landed in Denver.

Anyway, back to my story. Here we are in our first apartment. It's that first Monday morning where Wayne is off to his new job. Wayne told me when he woke up to go to work that day, he rolled over in bed, looked at me and thought, "What have I done?" He said that he wasn't doubting his love for me—that wasn't it. He was crazy about me. He says, "It was like I went to bed in those shiny, rented dress shoes and woke up in steel-toed boots all because of two words: "I do."" It was a shock for him. In fact, he words it like this: "I went from spectator to quarterback, from passenger to driver, from patient to doctor, from the dependent to the provider in one quick 'I do.'" Now we know that life changes for the bride, too, when we say, "I do," but for now we are looking at what our men experience as husbands. We're going to focus for the next few minutes on the husband's role, and what that feels like for him.

I want us to start out by looking at Ephesians 5, starting in verse 23, then going through the rest of the chapter. "Wives, be subject to your own husbands as to the Lord; for the husband is the head of the wife as Christ also is the head of the church, He Himself being the savior of the body. But as the church is subject to Christ, so also the wives ought to be to their husbands in everything." That word *ought* means "moral obligation," or, "they must." Verse 25 says, "Husbands, love your wives just as Christ also loved the church and gave Himself up for her, that He might sanctify her, having cleansed her by the washing of water with the word, that He might present to Himself the church in all her glory, having no spot or wrinkle or any such thing, but that she should be holy and blameless." So husbands *ought* (or *must*) also love their own wives as their own bodies. "He who loves his own wife loves himself; for no one ever hated his own flesh, but nourishes it and cherishes it just as Christ also does the church, because we are members of His body. For this cause a man shall leave his father and mother and shall cleave to his wife, and the two shall become one flesh. This mystery is great, but I am speaking with reference to Christ and the church. Nevertheless, let each individual among you also love his own wife even as himself, and let the wife see to it that she respect her husband."

In verse 32 he says, "I'm speaking with reference to Christ and the church." That's what he's describing here in this letter. He's using the marriage relationship, the husband and the wife, to describe Christ and the church because he knew his readers would understand that. So, when we remember that he's using "husband and wife" to describe Christ and the church, it's clear that God intended for marriage to be beautiful. We have let the world mess it up! We have the world telling us, "Marriage is a burden and is too difficult. Marriage will weigh you down." But that's not what God says. He intended for marriage to be a blessing.

When we look at verse 23, "The husband is the head of the wife as Christ also is the head of the church, He Himself being the savior of the body." When I think of my Jesus, He's everything to me. He's everything! Without Jesus, we would have no hope. Without Jesus, we would have no purpose. Without Jesus, we're lost. God explains the husband's role in the same way. When the husband says I do, he becomes the savior of the body, just as Christ is for the church. When we think of our husbands, striving to be godly men, wanting to do what God has asked them to do, God says, "You're going to be her savior." That's a massive responsibility!

Wayne had been raised in a godly home but he was 21 when we got married. I expected him to know how to do that for me from the beginning, forgetting that he'd never done it before and had no idea what that looked like for me. Wayne at least had a pattern to look at. So many of our husbands haven't been raised in Christian homes. They have been called to be the savior of the body, having **no idea** what that even looks like. Some of your husbands may not even know Jesus yet. Be patient; God is powerful!!

He's been called to be the savior of the body; that's a lot of responsibility on our men. You can see why some of them will say, "Okay, I've got this. I've got this," and then begin to say, "I can't do this! I can't do this!" Then, they find it's easier to coast through life. Remember the pressure they bear to be this godly man **for us**. They've been called to be the savior of the body.

Then drop down to verse 25, "Husbands, love your wives just as Christ also loved the church and gave Himself up for her." This is one of those looking back moments. When Wayne and I were dating, he had a very special car. I don't know car names, but it was a nice, brown, two-door car that he really loved. He sank lots of money in this car, fixed it up, and kept it spotless. It was one of those cars in which you had to be careful; if you were going to eat in it, you didn't dare drop a fry, because he was watching you like a hawk. He would wash it once a week. Some of you younger people don't know this, but they used to take stuff in a tub and wipe it on the car, and then they would buff it off. It's called waxing. You do that now when you drive through a machine. He loved that car! In fact, when we moved to Denver, we had to tow the car on a trailer because he didn't want to put the miles on his baby.

This is the looking back part. I can remember in the first apartment that we lived in, looking out of the window, down into the parking lot, and seeing that car. It was filthy and the top was peeling. I can remember judging him harshly, thinking, "He's not even taking care of his car anymore. He's just letting it fall apart." The inside was dirty too. You know how it is with kids. The whole, "Give-him-a-bottle-of-ketchup-if-it-will-keep-him-quiet" thinking. I didn't stop and really look at what was going on. Not realizing that he was laying himself aside for me. He didn't have the money or the time anymore—because he was giving himself up for me, for my marriage, for his family. He was having to put those things aside. I can think of other ways he made sacrifices, he laid himself aside for me, and I didn't even realize what he was doing.

Again, as I go through this discussion, please, if your husband isn't doing this, be patient. If you're thinking, *"His toys mean more to him than I do,"* then lift him up in prayer. Be patient. He may not know how. Our God is the creator. He can work in their hearts. So, they lay down their lives for us.

I love verses 26 and 27: "That He might sanctify her, having cleansed her by the washing of water with the word, that He might present to Himself the church in all her glory, having no spot or wrinkle or any such thing, but that she should be holy and blameless." This goes back to that idea of being the savior of the body. We have the husband as the head and the wife as the dangling body. I sometimes know that Wayne is turned one direction and I am turned in the other. Wayne's been commanded to keep me holy and blameless, to keep me without spot or wrinkle. I told you, my personality has me behaving like a spaz sometimes, and Wayne's saying, "I'm trying to keep you holy and blameless." That's a lot. That is so much!

Then in verse 29, another part of their role is mentioned. I love this: "For no one ever hated his own flesh, but nourishes it and cherishes it just as Christ also does the church." Now, I can remember as a young wife, looking at this and saying, "Oh, that is so romantic. I love that!" I have it underlined, highlighted, and circled. I can remember saying, "Look, Wayne. Look. You're going to nourish and cherish me. Isn't that beautiful? Wayne, look. You're going to—Hey! Have you **ever** read this in your life? You're supposed to be nourishing and cherishing me!" I can remember crying over this and thinking, "You aren't doing that for me. You aren't meeting my needs. You're not making me feel nourished and cherished."

We have to keep the thought in context. If you look in verse 28 God says, "So husbands ought also to love their own wives as their own bodies. He who loves his own wife loves himself; for no one ever hated his own flesh, but nourishes and cherishes it, just as Christ also does the church." This says that our husbands will nourish and cherish us like they do their own bodies. I don't know about you, but my body speaks to me. I know when I'm hungry, because I have a growling stomach. And I have a loud, growling stomach! I had a little girl sit with me one time during worship service, and I take that little, tiny crumb of cracker, that sip of juice, and my stomach starts urging, "More, more!" This little girl's eyes grew wide—she looked up at me and asked, "Was that a lion?" I was hungry, and the little bite of food made it even worse. My body speaks to me.

I know when I'm thirsty—in this phase of my life, I dehydrate easily so I require tons of water or I get dizzy and can even pass out. Life is bizarre as you get older. You young women get ready!! Menopause is another topic we don't talk about. Anyway, my body speaks to me and I know yours does too. So, our husbands have been commanded to take care of us as they would their own bodies. And they're looking at us saying, "I don't know. I don't know what I'm doing here. I'm male, remember." Many times we are telling them, "Well, if you loved me, you would know what my needs are." We think, *"If he loved me, he would know how to care for me. We've been married 6 months, he should know that about me."* They don't know what to do! They might say, "I'm going to give you some flowers, and here's some candy. How's that?" Because that's what the world is telling them nourishes us and cherishes us. That's not my personality. Poor Wayne! He didn't know what he was getting into. Wayne would bring me flowers and chocolate. Now, I never turn down chocolate. Never! I am the one that pokes a hole in the bottom of all of the candies in one of those boxes of assorted chocolates, so just give me a bag of M&M's. But, he'd bring flowers and put them on the table. I finally had to let him know in a loving manner that when he did that, all I see in my head is our love just wilting and dying there on the table for $50. That's how I see that. I had to let him know that's not the best way to meet my need. The year that he got me the Shark steam mop for Valentine's Day was the best! That met my needs. He finally got me! Now, we change over the years and I've changed my thinking a little bit. We were in Lowe's or Home Depot recently and they had their fall flowers out. I told Wayne that I wanted one for the front porch. He looked at me as if I had lost my mind and said, "I thought you didn't like flowers." I'm good with flowers; I just want them in a pot of dirt. I like that it takes me longer to kill them. But we're all different! Until you tell them what your needs are, they don't know! They are different than we are. You have to communicate with them, because they have been commanded to nourish and cherish us as they would their own bodies. We need to remember that they're trying to do what they must do for us, but they're not real sure what that even looks like.

In verse 31 he says, "For this cause a man shall leave his father and mother and shall cleave to his wife, and the two shall become one flesh." We all understand the "leave and cleave" part. If you are putting your parents **before** your husband, you need to stop it. Now, if he's putting his parents **before** you, he needs to stop as well. But remember, you can't change him. Find a time when you can express how you see that happening. Be careful of your words; don't be condemning. Let him know your perspective but be open to his.

You can read commentary after commentary on what the "one flesh" part means. What I see in my studies is that one flesh means there is one head, one body—there is one flesh, one life. That's what you become. It's about building one life—together.

That's a lot. So many times, you have this 19-year-old to whatever age he might have been when he married, saying, "You want me to lead this home? I don't even know how!" So you have to be patient with him. He takes over this large spiritual responsibility when he says, "I do." It's just huge! He's a godly man who is striving. Or maybe he doesn't have a relationship with Jesus, yet. We can see how sometimes it's easier to float. It's easier to just get through day to day.

When you stop and think about the difference between how men and women think, it should help you be more patient with him. A man's spiritual role is not going to look like women might think it should look. We're more emotional. We might say, "Oh, we should pray about that," or "Oh, hug her; she's hurting!" Men aren't that way. They think differently. Their spiritual leadership role may not actually look the way we have pictured it would in our minds because they're men. We need to remember that.

When a man says, "I do," he becomes the protector. In Genesis 3:16, Adam and Eve have been in the garden. They have sinned, and God turns to give them the consequences of that sin. He turned to Eve, saying, "Yet your desire shall be for your husband, and he shall rule over you." Now, God had been their protector prior to this. In the garden, God had been the One who was there for them. They had no worries whatsoever; they didn't even have to do laundry. Now they were being sent out. Eve had stepped in front of Adam where the fruit was concerned—she took the lead. God is telling her that she may want to continue to do that, but Adam is now in charge; Adam is going to be the one that stands and protects her.

I shared my personality with you. I'm not really afraid of anything. My fear used to be spiders, but then I had five kids. The first 4 are boys. I was finding my boys screaming like a girl when they saw a spider and I decided that was **not** a good thing. I had to conquer that fear.

I'm not afraid of people; in fact I am a people person. I'll talk to anyone, anywhere. I've learned to control that a little better because my children told me it was creepy to join the conversation of strangers from the bathroom stall. I **love** to hear the different life stories from people! Everyone has a story. When I see the homeless, I'm always wondering what their story is. What has happened in their lives to put them where they are at? Wayne and I would be in downtown Denver at night for dinner and I would be chasing a homeless person down the alley. "Excuse me, sir. Can I talk with you?" Wayne would have to remind me that I was putting myself in danger. Oops!

I have a sarcastic tongue in my mouth. I have learned some self-control on that. But through the years, it has been a struggle. If we were out to dinner and I saw a couple in which a man was treating a woman badly, something would come out of my mouth along the lines of "Oh, you must love her so much to treat her like that." Wayne would look at me like, *"What are you doing?"* Or, if the woman was being ugly to the man it would be, "I bet you treat your puppy better than that." Again, Wayne's eyes would get huge! I have grown up; I have learned to better control my tongue.

We lived in a little apartment in a bad part of town during the heating and air conditioning years. We weren't making very much money, which wasn't a big deal. We'd made it our home. I loved that little apartment! Upstairs there lived a woman with a four or five-year-old little boy, and she would live with man after man. I felt sorry for her because she didn't know Jesus. Well, one night I could hear her fighting with whomever she was living with at the time. Now I don't judge people for arguing loudly: Wayne and I are very vocal. But, I could hear crashing and I could hear that little boy crying. I don't remember exactly what was going on, but Wayne was distracted. I think someone else was there. I remember giving him the look that said, *"Are you going to do something about this?"* Well, he wasn't even aware any of this was going on, so finally I thought,

"*Okay, fine.*" I went upstairs and knocked on the door and this giant, angry man opened the door and said, "What!" I backed up a little and said, "I just want you to know I can hear you up here, and I'm worried about (the little boy). If it doesn't stop, I'm going to call the police." He slammed the door in my face, but I went back downstairs feeling **so** proud of myself. I came back into the apartment, and Wayne was standing there and said, "What did you do?" He said, "Tami, you're going to get me beat up. I want to protect you. I will protect you. But your behavior keeps throwing me out in front of a bus." In my mind, I'm thinking, *"But I'm Superwoman! I got this. I can take care of myself."* But, he's thinking, *"I'm the protector! Don't you understand? Whatever would happen to you, I have to step in the path to protect you."* I never thought about it that way. And it took me a while to understand, because I kept thinking, *"I've got this, I've got this."* Someone once said, "It's hard to protect a tornado." I love that. They're wanting to be the knights in shining armor. We need to remember that they've been called to protect us, and we have to allow them to do that.

Men have a **male** lobe in their brain that tells them they are to protect us from other areas too. Wayne wants to protect me from things like stopped up toilets. He doesn't want me to have to mess with it…and I let him! He also wants to protect me by taking care of all of those fix-it projects around the house, like a vacuum that's not working. Men are just weird.

They're also trying to protect us in spiritual ways. They've got this "holy and blameless, without spot or wrinkle" responsibility. It may be that you've heard your husband say, "I heard them announce a ladies' class at church—I thought you might be interested in that." What if you were to come back saying, "Ah, it's just the old ladies. I've studied that; I don't need that. Anyway, why would I want to spend one of my evenings doing that?" He's thinking, *"Holy and blameless, without spot or wrinkle."* Or he hears that the ladies' retreat is coming. "I thought that might be good for you. You might like that. I'll keep the kids. Or you could influence the younger women," he might say. You're thinking, *"If you're going to keep the kids, I'm going to go do something fun."* Or *"I do not sleep on bunkbeds."* He's thinking, *"Holy and blameless…I'm trying to be the protector. I'm trying to do that for you."* He's not going to tell you that! But, he's striving to keep you holy and blameless. He may mention some character trait that you may be showing that has him concerned. Maybe you are being influenced by the people at work and not **being** an influence. We can get very defensive because we think they are being judgmental or critical. They're the protector, physically and spiritually. How should they handle that? That's a lot for our husbands. Now, I know we are all responsible for our own souls. I'm not going to get into Heaven on the coattails of my husband. His faith is not going to get me there. But, when I read Scripture, it makes me consider that when Wayne stands before God, God will say, "Did you do everything you could to keep her holy and blameless?" This thinking makes me stop and remember that our husbands have been called to be our protectors and are trying to figure out what that looks like.

Next, when he says, "I do," he becomes the provider. Keep reading! I'm not saying that there is anything sinful with a woman working outside the home. That's not **at all** what I'm saying! I have done that. But the husband has been called to be the provider. We go back to Adam and Eve. God now turns to Adam to give him his consequence. "By the sweat of your face you shall eat bread" (Genesis 3:17-19). Adam would have to work for food! Here they had been in the garden **picking** their food, saying, "Oh, here, let's eat this!" Life was so easy for them! And now God says, "You're going to have to work for your food." 1 Timothy 5:8 says, "If anyone does not provide for his own and especially for those of his household, he has denied the faith and he is worse than an unbeliever." So the man has been called to be the provider. I'm not naive; I understand that living in this world today is expensive and often takes both of us working to just eat and have a roof over our heads.

We need to remember that often men have a picture in their heads of what that provision is going to look like. I had a young husband with a handful of children bring this into the light for me. He and his wife both were working and had made some changes for her to go part time until all the kids were in school. I was happy for their transition and asked him how it was going. He gave a heavy sigh and told me that he felt so guilty. He said, "Women aren't the only one with a "white picket fence" dream in their heads. I saw my wife being able to stay home with our babies and we can't afford to do that. I don't make enough. I can't make enough." I worked to encourage him with my words, then started asking men again about the aspect of provider. Most of them started with how difficult it is.

Let us make sure as women that we are careful of not focusing on material possessions in our homes. The world has really, really done a good one on us. It has convinced us that we all need to own a home, that we all need two cars, that we all need a lot of physical things. God tells us that with food and covering we will be content.

If you teach that to little kids, saying, "Okay, this says here in 1 Timothy 6:8 that with food and covering I'll be content. What is food?" They will start naming all their favorite foods; pizza, macaroni and cheese, chocolate cake. I agree with the chocolate cake—I've been known to eat that for breakfast. If you say, "Okay, what is covering?" Perhaps they will name a blankie, their jammies, or they'll say, "My clothes; my house." Children get it! I believe this is part of what God is meaning when He says, "And you will be as the little children." When we behave like, we get confused. Because we live in a world that tells us, "You need to have, you need to have, you need to have, you need to have!" We keep putting this pressure on ourselves and on our families.

We hear so often about being a cheerful giver and how we're supposed to give in 2 Corinthians 9:7. We need to read the rest of the chapter. Verse 8 says, "You are given so that you are provided for every good work." Or verse 11 in which Paul says, "You are given so that you may give liberally." The reason we are given material things is so we can share them with others. Often we become hoarders. *"I have this nice house, I have this nice furniture...never had anybody over, never done anything with it."* We're hoarders, and we need to be careful of that. I had an older woman tell me one time that she couldn't have the young families over because she had new carpet and didn't want anything spilled on it. At that very moment I promised myself to never put the value of my material possessions before the value of people.

Our husbands are carrying this role of provider. And so many times we don't even think about what we say to them. I've been there, done that. When Wayne and I lived in Denver we would go to the Parade of Homes. I loved doing that!

It doesn't affect me in the slightest, because it's pretend. I go through those multi-million-dollar homes, saying, "Oh, look. Isn't this fun? I could make that. Take a picture of it. (Then I never make anything.) The whole church could come in here, or we could have all the kids over for a holiday—this would be so fun!", never thinking anything about it. I'm in a pretend world. But, Wayne's hearing, *"And you will never give this to me."*

Or we'll walk through a toy store and I'll see one of those life-size cars that little kids drive around and I'll say, "Wouldn't Sawyer love that?" Wayne says there is a lobe in his brain that hears, *"And you can't provide that for my grandchildren."* I'm not thinking that way at all! We have 10 grandchildren; I know that isn't happening. But Wayne is thinking *"I could hardly provide for my own children and now it continues with my grandchildren."* We need to be careful with our words! Your husband is trying to be the provider.

You may be working and love your job. That's fantastic! I'm finding more or more families where the wife is actually making more money than the husband. What a blessing that is to your family! Just be careful of your thinking. Remember that it's not **your** money, but it belongs to the **one flesh**. But, also be careful with saying something like, "Man, I hate my job. What I'd give if I could just stay home." He's hearing, *"And if you made more money I could."* So be careful, ladies. They've got this huge, huge role that God has given them. We can lift them up and let them know it's okay. **We can do this together. We have to do it together**. Let them know and encourage them. Make sure the focus is where it needs to be.

So, here are the men, and they've been called to the role of being the spiritual leader of our homes. That's a lot! I feel sorry for them when I pause and think about the weight of their role. I often thank God I'm not a man. They've been called to be our protectors. Just look around—that's not easy. They've been called to be the provider in a world that is telling us that we never have enough. That's hard!

I say our role is to help them into Converse. But Converse aren't comfortable--I have gel inserts in mine. That's what we want to be for our husbands, a gel insert in their shoes, to make their journey easier. I don't want to be a wife kicking rocks into his shoes and making it **more** difficult for him. Or I find myself sometimes trying to push him out of his shoes so that I can walk in them for him.

Remember that your husband loves you. He picked you. He loves you. Remember that! He may not be expressing it the way you would like him to express it. You may not see it on his face when he looks at you. But he loves you.

Are they going to make mistakes? They're not perfect. We make mistakes, too! I don't want Wayne keeping tally of my mistakes and throwing them back at me. I don't want that, because it would be continual—I am a flawed person. We all are. Sometimes our husbands will make less-than-perfect decisions, maybe early in marriage, and we kind of unintentionally rub it in if we're not careful. "I thought we'd buy a new car. Remember that time you bought that lemon?" And he's thinking, *"You think I don't remember the consequences of my bad mistake?"* Or, perhaps he's made a financial decision—or you made a financial decision together—early in your marriage with consequences that hold on for a long, long time, and you're second-guessing him. We need to be forgiving and patient with them. They're going to make mistakes. We all do. We need to be forgiving and forgetting. Lift them up!

Remember when you're faced with great difficulty, when you have hurtful things going on in your life like loss of a job, sickness, family problems: they're hurting, too. I know all of you have your stories. Wayne and I over the last few years have gone through difficulties with our children—hurtful, hurtful things we never dreamed would happen. One night, I was up in the bathtub. My hour-long bath is my alone time. It is also my time to cry. I've heard many women say the shower is their time to cry. That's what I was doing. I was in the bathtub having an **ugly** cry. The door opened and Wayne came in, asking, "Are you okay?" "What are you doing in here?" I asked. He looked startled. He said, "What's wrong with you? Are you okay?" "I'm fine. I just needed to cry. It's just—you know—I'm hurting." I shared what I was feeling at the moment. He said, "Okay, all right. As long as you're okay." I assured him I would be fine, that he could just let me cry.

Well, a few weeks later, I had come down from my bath early, and Wayne was sitting on the couch, crying. "Did somebody call?" I asked. "What is it? Is somebody dead?" Wayne doesn't cry so I thought something awful had happened. But he looked up, and said, "I'm hurting, too. I'm hurting, too, Tam." He's the man, and he is carrying the load. Usually we are the ones saying, "Would you hold me? I just hurt. I hurt so bad!" And they want to do that for us, to help us through. Remember, in difficult times they are hurting, too. So we need to be patient with them. Just because they aren't responding the way we think that they should, remember they hurt, too.

They're striving to be godly husbands. Wayne voiced it this way. He'll lay down his head at night and think, *Did I say too much today? Was I too controlling over her today? Or did I say too little? Does she know I love her? Did I do too much today, or did I do too little?* He said, "It's overwhelming to me. I hope you know I love you." They don't always voice it. They're wired differently than we are. They don't always show it. But they love us.

Let's consider our husbands and the role to which God has called them. Let's be patient with them. I know it can be disappointing when things happen. It hurts us. I understand that. But, sometimes it helps me to look back at him and set my feelings aside. I can look back at him and say, "That has to be so hard!" We can pray for our men. We know that the responsibility that they carry can be overwhelming for them, because our role can be overwhelming for us as well. Remember the responsibility that they carry on their shoulders. I had one young man tell me, "If I don't work, we don't eat. If I don't protect, we're in danger. If I don't lead, then we are all lost. So much rests on me. They're all counting on me."

With God's help, we can help them see their strengths. Men can be hard on themselves because they feel so inadequate. As women, we can lift them up, we can encourage them. Let them know that we appreciate the things that they do for us. We can acknowledge the fact that they are trying. We can be women who are positive thinkers, striving to make our marriages a blessing not just to us, but to our husbands as well!

- Share what makes you feel "nourished and cherished."

- What can you do in your "spiritual walk" to allow room for your husband to be your spiritual protector? To help you be "holy and blameless, without spot or wrinkle"?

- What does "materialism" look like? Are you caught up in materialism? You will pass this on to your children. They will go into marriage **focused** on material possessions. They start out with that stress in their marriages.

- Focus on your husband's strengths! Make a list if you need to. This will help keep you in a positive frame of mind.

CHAPTER 7

TONGUE TIED: IMPROVING YOUR COMMUNICATION

Your marriage has been marked by communication. The relationship has been an ongoing conversation. The conversation may have begun by asking someone, "Hey, I need you to find out from her friend if she thinks I'm cute." Or maybe you passed a handwritten note to a friend saying, "I need you to find out from his friend if he likes me." Maybe it was a more grown-up conversation in which one of you finally built up the courage and said, "Hey, I wonder, would you like to go for coffee?" or "Would you like to go to the movies?" It was the beginning of a much larger conversation in which grew in your interest for one another.

Then, you came up to one of those important conversations in which he said, "Wouldn't you like to be my wife?" Or she said, "Wouldn't you like me to be your wife?" (Whichever way that worked out.) Then there was that dialogue in which you made a commitment on your wedding day. You said, "I do," and she said, "I do," or "I will" and "I will." All of that conversation has been going on in your marriage. It has been part of your marriage virtually from the very beginning, and it is a part of your marriage even if there is no communication going on, because it is impossible to **not** communicate. The question is, are you communicating what needs to be communicated?

Good communication is paramount to a marriage's success. At the same time, poor communication can be destructive. In fact, unhealthy communication may be the biggest problem any couple faces. The reason communication comes to the top of my list of marital problems is this: First, when a couple doesn't communicate well with each other, the relationship struggles. Second, poor communication contributes to almost every other problem (or interferes with the resolution of those problems). If there's a problem with money, but the communication isn't good, guess what? The problem gets worse. If the problem has to do with parenting and communication isn't good, there are even bigger problems ahead. If there has been unfaithfulness, poor communication can prevent repentance, forgiveness, and the rebuilding of trust. If communication can be improved in our marriages, it will help us avoid many problems and give us a tremendous resource for finding solutions to other problems. Tami and I don't have communication problems. We just have to keep the neighbors across the street from hearing it. That's all we have to worry about. The truth is every couple can improve their communication, no longer how long they have been married.

The tongue is a powerful thing. Some suggest it is the most powerful muscle in the human body. Tami says it is because I exercise it more than any other muscle. That may be true, physiologically speaking, but it is powerful in other ways as well. James, the half-brother of Jesus, writes about the power of the tongue (James 3:1-12). This is how he describes it (paraphrased):

> The tongue is like a rudder on a ship. It is small, but it can direct by its movement the entirety of the ship (life). It is like a fire, but not a good fire that warms those who are cold. It is a fire that is out of control, and it can destroy wherever it is set loose, a fire that defiles the entire body. It's a double-edged sword that can bless God with one breath and then curse those who are around us, those who God made with the next. The tongue really is a reflection of the heart, because you don't get good water from a bad fountain, and bad water doesn't come out of a good fountain.

If you can manage the tongue, you have and can manage just about anything else, because it is difficult to control our tongues. It is most certainly powerful.

We know this to be true about the tongue and about the power of words. Anyone who has been on the receiving end of some verbal abuse can affirm that. Communication can hurt. Like the "sticks and stones may break your bones," they told me when I was a little short kid in high school, "but words can never harm you." That's not always true. Though I learned to laugh off the quips about being a "pip-squeak," a "pee-wee," and a "shorty," I can tell you now that those things hurt. They eat at you. You learn to get through them, maybe, but they're painful. In the same way that words can heal, they can really hurt. Sometimes they hurt even more than a physical strike, and most certainly can be longer lasting. In our society we even have even minimized some words to a letter, the "N-word" or the "F-word," recognizing their damaging effects.

But somehow, we still think, "Well, you know what? I can say whatever to my spouse, and he or she knows I don't mean it, right? I mean, we love each other. They know I'm just 'kidding' (my wife hates that one)." You need to be very careful that you do not allow harmful words to come in and become part of your communication to each other—words that are hateful, vengeful, spiteful, reckless, uncaring, or angry. We need to take those things out of our vocabulary. I want to encourage you to be those who are slow to speak, thinking through your words before you say them, making them go through the sentry of your mind.

Often we might say something, then we think, "*I shouldn't have said it; but then I've already said it, and I'm going to have to back me.*" So, we say something else, or we retreat without apology. It is a powerful thing this thing called the tongue. And, as with any tool, we need to be careful that we don't cut our fingers off (or our spouses' either) while we're using it. I want to encourage you to work on getting that destructive, poisonous speech out of your communication. Here are some other ways you can improve the communication between you and your spouse.

LISTEN BETTER

I don't know if you know this, but we're not, as a people, very good listeners anymore. The human ear I'm told is actually more sophisticated than a dog's ear, but because our brain is so much more advanced, it quickly sorts through all the sounds and discards anything that is unnecessary. This can be seen in a husband who is watching the football game when his wife says, "The trash is full," and he fails to respond. He's concentrating on and only listening to the game. Again she comes back to the door of the family room and repeats her statement. "Honey, the trash is full." Finally, in the loving, caring way in which only a wife can express it, she states emphatically, **"Trash. Full."** The husband, seemingly coming out of anesthesia and with eyes still focused on the game, he finally says, "Huh?" One wife said she actually brought the trash can to the middle of the kitchen one day and said, "The trash is full." Her husband got up from his favorite game day recliner, headed right into the kitchen, saw the trash can and promptly went right around it on his way to the refrigerator for another soda. **So** much for trying to get him to take the hint. That's selective hearing.

We are not very good listeners. We have a tendency, especially when the argument is heated, to tune the other person out or to be preparing our rebuttal in our minds instead of listening. One time, Tami and I were having a "conversation": we were going back and forth making our case about how we should handle a specific situation. I was making my point and telling her how foolish hers was; she was making her point and telling me how foolish mine was. After about an hour of this going back and forth (yes, an hour), she indignantly asked, "Are you suggesting…?" I, equally agitated, responded, "I certainly am!!" She retaliated with a swift, "You can't suggest that, because that's what I'm suggesting." We realized we both had the exact same perspective on the situation, but we were trying so hard to make our point that neither one of us never actually listened to what the other one was saying. I heard of one couple who agreed to a rule at their house that whenever they're arguing, the winner of the argument is actually the first person who actually listens to the other one.

We need to learn to listen. But listening can be hard, especially if you are a talker like Tami's husband. Here is what has helped me. Maybe it will help you too. I learned a long time ago in sales that the one who asks questions controls the conversation. But asking questions has other benefits, too. For one thing, it allows us to clarify what the other person is saying. We become a better listener when our talking is in the form of questions. Maybe it's a question like,

"So, what I'm hearing you say is…?" Sometimes we need to be sure we know what's actually being said and what the real issue is. And asking a question allows that to happen. At the same time, asking questions shows the courtesy of being interested in what the other person thinks and has to say. "What do you think we should do?" "How do you see the problem?" "How do you think I am contributing to the problem or solution?" "How do you think you are contributing to the problem or solution?" You see, we begin show interest in their particular view. Then this courtesy, when returned, grants us permission to speak. Because once we've asked and allowed the other person to share what's on his or her mind, we then get our opportunity to share. Sometimes listening helps us hold our tongues until our brains kick in. A chance for our first thought to get a second look and to even cool our emotions a bit before we speak. Sometimes we are better off to allow some things to process before we speak. Pausing to listen helps.

Be aware of nonverbal communication while you are listening. My wife (by her own admission) and her face are at odds with one another sometimes. I know this because I will do something, and I might say, "You were displeased with that," and she'll say, "I didn't say anything." My response is, "No, but your face is shouting at me." They say that the human face can make up to 70,000 facial expressions. I'll just tell you, in my experience, most of them are negative. When non-verbal communication takes place, your spouse is listening with both of his or her eyes. With all those kinds of expressions, we are communicating even when we're not verbally communicating! And I'm afraid we're often telling the truth more with those body languages then when we're saying something with our mouths. We need to be aware of those things.

Part of the listening problem is that the spouse who is the talker just won't hush and the quiet one never says anything. That's not good listening on either person's part. One person so fills the conversation that the other cannot get a word in edgewise. Meanwhile the other is always silent; "processing" or pouting causes frustration and a communication barrier because a spouse doesn't know, **from his or her spouse**, what the other is thinking and feeling.

If you are the talker in your family, you would be well served to learn to hush (that's saying it politely). And if you are the spouse that rarely speaks up, you would do your marriage and your spouse a great service by speaking up on occasion. If both of you are talkers, like Tami and I are, well…pray.

DON'T JUST SHOW IT; SAY IT!

Now, when we talk about communication as a problem, we usually think we're only talking about bad communication. But bad communication doesn't just come in the form of bad words or bad conversation; bad communication can result simply because there's not enough good communication.

When your relationship began, there was probably a lot of good communication (although it may have been a bit clumsy). You communicated in little notes, in greeting cards, in telephone conversations, or, as is becoming more and more common, in text messages, emails, and the like. You start out having lots of good conversation. You talk about each other, what you like, what you have in common, what you want in life, what you think about things, and what your dreams are. You say things like, "That sounds great to me," "I love what you dream," "I love what you want to be," "I love what you want to do," and of course, "I love you." Then we get married and we start to put all of that regular, good conversation aside because things in life start getting in the way. We might even get to the point when we don't even take the time to say, "I love you." We might excuse that away in our own minds or our own defense by saying something like, "We've been together a long time and she (or he) knows that I love her even if I don't tell her."

I'm a big fan of Broadway musicals. There's a classic musical called *Fiddler on the Roof*. It's about a man who is wrestling with change. Times are changing, along with the traditional things with which he is familiar. He and his wife are the product of an arranged marriage. They had been married for some time, and one day he's become a bit reflective and he begins wondering if theirs is just an amiable arrangement or if there really is a relationship. In song he asks, "Golde, do you love me?" She replies, "Do I **what**?" "I'm asking you," he says, "do you love me?" She responds, "You're upset, you're worn out. Go inside, go lie down! Maybe it's indigestion." He pushes the issue and asks again, "Do you love me?" Her confusion and frustration blurts out a series of facts about their relationship, "For twenty-five years I've washed your clothes, cooked your meals, cleaned your house, given you children, milked the cow; after twenty-five years, why talk about love right now?" He asks again, "Yes, but do you love me?" She contemplates, "For twenty-five years I've lived with him, fought with him, starved with him, twenty-five years my bed is his. If that's not love, what is?" "So, you love me?" he gently asks one final time. Exasperated by the question, she surrenders her answer and reveals her real feelings, "I suppose I do." The song ends with a little grin and he responds, "I suppose I love you too. It doesn't change a thing. But even so after twenty-five years it's nice to know."

In other words, it's not just enough to see all the actions that show love. Sometimes it needs to be heard. **Say it**! At the same time, a love that is not paired with action is a hollow expression. We can't just say, "I love you," and then not do anything about it. But, let me just suggest to you that your marriage will benefit greatly by bringing good "I love you" language back into your relationship—not just to act like you love one another, but to say "I love you." It may be in a note, it may be a card, it may be a glance that is followed with a mouthed *I love you*. Here's some advice for men, you can mouth the words "*I'll have a few*" (regarding chocolate chip cookies), and it looks the same as "*I love you.*" So, use that as you see fit. Also, I want to discourage you from writing on the mirror some morning, "I love you," with your wife's lipstick. It may seem "romantic" at the moment, but at $20 a tube, her response will probably not be the response you had hoped for. Anyway....

Couples, you need to practice other good communications as well. You each need to say things like, "I appreciate you." Not just for something big or special that has been done, but for even the regular, simple, mundane and often overlooked tasks. Regularly saying, "I appreciate what you do this for our family," "I'm thankful to you and to God for you," "I am praying for you today" are some of those positive communications.

There are other positive expressions like, "I'm sorry." Not just, "I'm sorry you feel that way," but "I apologize for making you feel that way." The companion to that is, "I forgive you." Not just, "Well, we all said what we had to say and we let it go on, and now it's over." Take time to pause and say **verbally**, "I'm sorry," "I forgive you," "Let's move beyond this together." Positive communication is an essential part of any relationship. If you want a relationship to grow and thrive, you're going to have to re-interject that kind of positive communication to it. It's especially true in a marriage. Good positive communication is a must.

CREATE A COMMUNICATION SAFE ZONE

A safe zone is a setting in which you and your spouse can verbally exchange communication without the fear of retaliation. Now, that doesn't mean the rule is three rounds until the knockout. It simply refers to a setting in which someone can express himself without fear of reaction, saying "I have this concern...or I'm bothered by...or this is hurting my feelings." It is a place where you can talk openly, honestly, frankly, and fairly without the fear of reactionary retaliation. It's a place for mutual, mature conversation that a couple has come to by agreement, a place and time without other distractions, to say, "Let's talk about these things."

Maybe the best way to understand a safe zone is to understand some places that are not safe zones. For example, the end of the day is not a safe zone. Tami and I made a rule that after about 11 p.m. we don't talk about serious stuff unless it is absolutely necessary. Even if the conversation isn't about a difficulty, if it's heavy with information or decisions need to be made, it's not very productive. Neither one of us are really in the mood for a serious discussion and it doesn't get resolved before we go to bed. We're all worked up with it still on our minds and unresolved, and we wake up the next morning feeling beat to death! The end of the day is not the best time.

At the same time, first thing in the morning is not a very good safe zone. No one wants to wake up to his spouse saying, "Good morning, Sunshine... You know what? We've got some stuff we need to talk about!!!" (emphasis intended). Understandably some things may need discussed as you go about your day or before you each go your own separate ways. You may both be well rested, but there is a whole day ahead, and it has plenty of concerns for itself. This is probably not the best way to start the day. Because there are time constraints, the issue is left hanging, unresolved. You typically can't accomplish a great deal in a few moments as you ready yourself, ready the kids, ready for work, and ready for the day.

Right in the middle of a problem isn't a good safe zone either (or, as they say, "in the heat of battle"). It is not the safest communication zone when he left his dirty underwear in the middle of the floor, and the wife is asking, "Is that your underwear?" (His response might be, "I hope so." Problem fixed—there you go.) Whether it's the dirty underwear, or the dirty dishes, or how the kids are being treated, etc., etc., when tensions are high, it is not the best time to sit down and have a reasonable conversation about it.

A safe zone is not at the kitchen table with friends and family gathered for Thanksgiving Dinner or for that matter any public setting. It is not the place to address her inability to make gravy that does not "clot" or his failure to remember to fix the guest toilet. There may be a tendency to think that this public forum will give a "home field advantage" or moral support from those in attendance, but it is not the time to air your grievances. Large gatherings, the grocery store checkout lane, the church foyer, or the living room in front of the kids are not places for productive conversation. These are private conversations that require privacy. Now, I am not of the mindset that parents should never "fight in front of their children." I think at some point children need to learn how to "fight fair" and it needs to be seen in Mommy and Daddy. But let me just tell you right now, using them as pawns in your argument game of chess is not a good idea. Your safe zone needs to be a private setting.

You need to find a time—set specifically aside—maybe even with some written-out guidelines about where and how you are going to talk about your problems. You need to give each other the right and respect to be able to speak candidly, knowing you will not blow up, and in turn be given the same courtesy. That promotes good conversation and helps both partners in a marriage talk about their issues.

LEARN A NEW LANGUAGE...TOGETHER

Finally, I want to just suggest that you learn a new language together. The greatest struggle that men and women have is this: they speak two different languages. Now, I don't just mean the fact that Tami speaks Oklahoman and I speak English. She speaks "Woman" and I speak "Man" (and I speak it fluently and frequently). We are also two different individuals that think and communicate differently. Maybe I can illustrate it this way. When I was young my grandfather worked for the Holy Sugar Company. They grew, harvested, and processed white table sugar from sugar beets. His responsibility was the oversight of many of the crop fields, but he was not directly responsible for the Mexican farm workers. Still on occasion one of them would come by his house looking for their paycheck. I remember seeing him standing on his front porch. He could barely understand what they were asking and was even less able to communicate back to them. He would speak in what I suppose he thought was a Spanish accent and yell loudly in a broken and discombobulated combination of English and presumed Spanish word endings something like, "No checkie hereo!" Needless to say, they didn't get their check and he didn't get their point. In a similar way, spouses don't always speak or translate each other's language.

So, husbands spend their lives trying to learn to speak and understand woman (granted it is a confusing and complicated language). A wife spends her life trying to speak and understand man (a simple language of single syllable words and occasional grunts). So, they struggle communicating these two languages. They just end up yelling at each other from the porch. My proposal is to learn an entirely new language together!

I took a little bit of French in junior high, and I can still say three or four expressions, but I can't speak French. If Tami and I decided we were going to France and we wanted to be able to communicate the language, we would learn French together. She's a little bit better at linguistics, so she'd be a little bit ahead of me, but for the most part our vocabulary would be about the same because we'd be learning it together. And our ability to communicate in conversations that we learned together would be about the same. In other words, if I said something to her, like, "*Parlez vous francais?*" she would be able to respond to that because she and I had learned that expression together. (By the way, that means, "Do you speak French?" Learned that in jr. high). There would be very little that I said that she couldn't understand because we learned it together.

Now I'm not suggesting, however, that you learn Spanish, French, German, or even Chinese together. I am suggesting that you learn a new kind of language; it's a special God-given language. It is a language that you can learn together, and it begins to give you the same vocabulary, if you will—the same kind of expressions. It is a language that is described in 1 Corinthians 13, in that famous chapter on love.

Take a moment and replace the word *love* used in 1 Corinthians 13:4-7 with the phrase "our communication." I don't think that is being unfair to the text. Every expression of love found in this chapter are verbs. Verbs are action words, and since communication is an action, then our communication should have these loving characteristics. Listen what this new language sounds like.

"*Our communication is patient....*" Imagine if you were able to introduce into your conversation a language that could just wait? What if we gave our first impulse a second thought? What if we thought before we spoke? What if we paused before blurting out? What if our communication was filled with more listening than talking? What if our conversation became conversation that was more patient and thoughtful?

"*Our communication is kind....*" What if we had a communication that was always kind? I mean, certainly we'd take away all of those hateful and hurtful words. We'd remove the exaggerated words of hate and hostility, the words that tear down and don't build up, the words that are unkind and unfair.

"*Our communication is not envious or jealous....*" How about a communication that is not envious or jealous? Envious has that idea of wanting what someone else has. Envy thinks, "They have the advantage or they're getting the last word." So is our conversation when it is marred by envy. Envy is self-serving and selfish. With this new language we put that kind of selfish perspective aside.

"Our communication does not brag...." How about a communication that does not boast, *"I want, I like, I think, I believe, I don't like, I don't think."* Do you see the problem? It's an "I" problem. It is all about **me** being the first, the best...and truthfully, the only. Boastful communication is all about winning the argument or showing our superiority.

"Our communication doesn't act unbecomingly...." Consider a communication that is not rude, that is not coarse. I know of couples who have beautiful speech. They typically talk nicely to everyone—until they get in an argument. Then the gates are opened with language that would make even the toughest man blush. I mean, it all comes out. This speech is directed at their spouses, the ones who they claim to love the most. Well, our new conversation model simply will not allow that kind of language in our speech.

"Our communication does not seek its own...." Better said, "Gets its own way." We want communication that is not self-seeking—conversation that is not focused on me but focused on "we." It would be self-sacrificing and more concerned about seeking the well-being of another over ourselves.

"Our communication is not easily provoked...." The idea here is that love isn't overly sensitive, it doesn't get its feeling hurt at every little thing, it's not easily set off. What if we could just employ communication that is similar? What if we were not so quick tempered or easily angered? Sometimes we're like a race car, going from 0 to 60 in 3.5 seconds! What if we could defuse that and say, "You know what, I am just not going to get angry when we talk?"

"Our communication does not take into account a wrong suffered...." I love this one (or hate it). How about communication that does not keep a record? Think about taking out the garbage. Would you ever bring it back in? I wouldn't think so. Keeping a record is like saying, "We're going to put that trash-filled argument bag over here in the corner then the next time we have an argument, we're going to burst out that rotten, maggot-infested filth that we put aside a long time ago (if it's to your advantage). That's what we are doing when we say things like, "Well, you told me the last time..." or "You said when this happened

before…" or "Do you remember…?" The better communication says there's no record. We'll address this one thing, here and now, and that's the extent of it.

"Our communication does not rejoice in unrighteousness…but rejoices in truth…." A communication that does not delight in evil—what does that mean? Have you ever seen a couple who argue (or maybe you've been that couple who argues) and one person is actually glad the other spouse is wrong, because it just fuels the fire of how right the first one is? We actually are glad they're wrong. Otherwise, we would have to agree. We don't want to agree. We want to go on and on about this until the other person concedes and shouts, **"You're right! I'm wrong!"** We then find ourselves delighting in evil, even if we are actually in the wrong.

Instead, how about a communication that rejoices in truth rather than rejoicing in being right? In other words, what if the objective of our conversations were not to prove my case right or your case wrong (or, in reverse, your case right and mine wrong)? It would be a communication says, "We want to find out what is right, what is true, and we'll pursue that."

"Our communication bears, believes, and hopes all things…." How about a communication that protects, trusts, hopes, and endures (perseveres)? Imagine if we could create that kind of language in our marriages. Our families, our schools, and our streets? How different our world would be?

I'll give you an exercise. I want you as a couple to take a piece of paper and write down each of these characteristics found in 1 Corinthians 13. Look at the list and ask yourselves, "What does communication that is patient, kind, etc. look like?" Or when you're going round and round, ask yourselves, "Is this patient? Is this kind? Is this boasting? Is this rude? Is this self-seeking or holding a grudge?"

If you really want to improve the communication in your relationship, learn this new love language. It's one that is suitable and fitting for a couple who is growing in their relationship. It will not only fix the current communication model, but it will also begin to solve any other problems that may exist in your marriage and other relationships as well.

CHAPTER 8

SHOELESS: INTIMACY IN MARRIAGE (FROM A HUSBAND)

This is one of the hardest lessons I've ever had to publicly speak about. I have done my own father's funeral, and I have done the funeral of a really good friend who died unexpectedly of a heart attack at 48. I have done a funeral of a friend, a young wife and mother who took her own life. You can give me five-minutes warning and put me an auditorium of 50,000 people, and I will talk my fool head off. I might not have anything to say but I'd be totally at ease. None of that presents me as much difficulty as does this particular discussion, because it is on intimacy in marriage. I am not going to be so presumptuous as to come into your bedroom, and I'm not inviting you into mine, but I do want you to understand intimacy from a Biblical perspective.

Guys don't typically talk about intimacy in marriage to anyone. They don't talk to their wives about it. They don't really talk to their buddies about it. If a man ever does talk about intimacy, he does from one of two perspectives. Men talk about it from the biology lab, the health class, or the doctor's office. They approach the subject clinically, giving everything a medical name. And, for the most part, they're comfortable with that. Or, in the locker room, on the playground, or at some sporting event, men may talk about it, giving every part of intimacy some slang, crude, crass definition. Then they kind of nudge their buddy and say, "Get it? Huh? Do ya?"

Right now, I wish that I could just roll a series of charts and coloring sheets out about the anatomy of men and women, put my glasses on the end of my nose, and say, "Now, the human body is designed like this." That would be great. There's even a temptation to try to get away with telling a dirty joke and we could all giggle and get past the subject (I know that would be inappropriate). I think however that there is a more productive approach.

Every married couple is different. We find some marriages in which sexual intimacy is more important to the man than it is to the woman. On the other hand, we also find some in which sexual intimacy is more important to the woman than it is to the man. My hope is that between what I share with you and what Tami shares in the next chapter, you will be encouraged to talk with your spouse. Together, consider your relationship and how all of these things apply to you.

It has been my experience that, for the most part, sexual intimacy is at its peak right after marriage. We are young, and we're excited about the new relationship. Young men still have hormones that are raging (and some girls too), and they finally find a place to express themselves sexually. There are no kids, there is less work-related stress, and the problems of life are minimal—sexual intimacy is the fashion.

But, somewhere along the way, sexual intimacy falls out of fashion. And typically—not in every relationship, but generally speaking—it is the man who begins to say, "What happened? We used to have sex a lot more. And now it just doesn't seem to be very important." He may even be tempted to find some other outlet, such as pornography or even adultery. That's not the right way to interpret it and certainly not the way to deal with it. I want you to understand a little more about sexual intimacy. I think it will help when sex isn't as regular as it used to be or as regular as you'd like it to be.

Let's start with this (and this is the good news). Sex is an important part of a healthy marriage. When it is absent a marriage can struggle.

There was a couple who were high-end attorneys in New York City, and they were being interviewed about how they made two careers work. In the conversation it came out from one of them that they put intimacy in their calendar: "This is the night that we're going to have sex." The interviewer said,

"That doesn't seem very romantic." And the lady responded, "Well, here's the thing. Everything in our life that's important finds its way onto our calendar: our appointments, our meetings, our clients, grooming the dog, having our hair done, having the cars serviced, and parties. Any kind of occasion finds its way onto our calendar if it's important. This is an important part of our marriage, so we're going to have to work to make it part of it."

It may not be very romantic about it if your wife comes in, and leans over and says, "Hey, I just want you to know you're my 8:30 p.m. tomorrow night." That's probably not going to be the way to approach it. The idea is that as a couple you need to be intentional about sex. It's that's important.

At our house we say, "It's Friday." That's our little code for "How about tonight?" I can tell you right now that there have been times in which there were no Fridays in a week. I don't know why that is. I look on my calendar. It says Wednesday, Thursday, but somehow we skip right over to Saturday. There have been times in which Tami says, "I guess Friday's going to have to be on Monday." I can also tell you there have been some months that didn't have any Fridays for any number of reasons. And every now and then, I get surprised and there's more than one Friday in a week (I was so excited about Joel Osteen's book called *Every Day Is Friday*; but, it's not what I thought it was, so I returned it).

God made men and women as sexual beings. In Genesis 1:27 Moses writes the words of God, "Let Us make mankind in Our image, according to Our likeness." Moses continues his record of the creation event in the next verse, "So God created man in His own image, in the image of God He created him; male and female He created them." Did you see that? He created them "male" and "female." Those are sexual designations. God intended for husband and wives to go together sexually. He created us physically different so as to complement one another in the sexual relationship.

God has created us the way He did for a reason! He created us differently physically. Most of you figured this out by the time you were about four years of age. You were dropped in a bathtub with a sister or with a cousin and one of you asked, "Why doesn't she have a...?" or that cousin asked, "Why does he have a...?" Then someone yanked you out of the tub, and there was never another boy/girl bath. Boys and girls are different. Personally, I am glad that my wife does not look like a man. I am glad that she is a woman. I believe that God has created in man a desire for woman. Her shape, her personality, and sometimes the things that are the most frustrating to us men about a woman are really what we like. Men and women are different on the outside.

We also need to understand that men and women are different on the inside as well. We are wired differently. Let me illustrate it this way. I asked Tami, "Do me a favor. I've been using these shoe analogies for our seminars. If intimacy were a shoe, if I could explain to the men, 'This is how a wife views intimacy,' what shoe would it be?" (Why I needed a shoe illustration for something that usually occurs in bare feet, I'm not sure). I figured she would say something like, "A red, sexy high heel shoe. Instead, she said, "Well, it would be a 'fun shoe.'"

"A fun shoe? What's a fun shoe?" I thought. She continued, "They're **fun** shoes. It's the pair we buy for a special occasion. It's the one that's shiny and glittery. We go out on a dinner date and it's **the** shoe for the occasion. That's what it is. It's about us being together." I didn't understand it fully. Then she added, "As one woman put it, '*Intimacy* means Into Me You See.'" "*Okay, I think I get it...I think.*" Then I said "Okay, how about a man? If you were to describe how a man thinks about intimacy, what shoe would it be?" She said quickly without any hesitation, "A Nike tennis shoe!" I asked her why. She answered, "What's their slogan?" Oh...**Just Do It!**

In other words, for a woman, intimacy is primarily about relationship, and for a guy (at least from the woman's perspective) it's...Just Do It. That gave me some insight as to how they view us as well. Like I said before, this isn't always the case but often is. Women can be all about the physicality of sex and men can more emotional than we often think. I've seen guys, 75,000+ of them at a football game, scream their fool heads off. We're emotional guys. We're just wired differently and often express it differently.

Maybe this will help you understand the difference in the wiring of a man and a woman (pun intended as you'll see). On the wall is a switch that operates the lights. If I were to stand next to it and say, "Lights on!" and wait for that light to turn on. I could yell at that light switch all day and night, and it wouldn't work. So I call my electrician friend, "Hey, I need you to come to my place and fix a broken light switch." When he gets there he asks, "What's wrong?" and I say, "This light switch doesn't work. It's broken. Let me show you." I repeat my vocal commands, "Lights on!" He would look at me like I was crazy. He would start asking me if I have some kind of a problem. Then he would probably walk over and flip the light switch to see if it worked. Surprise! It comes right on.

Now imagine if I were to say, "Yeah, yeah but I don't want to operate it like that. I want to be able to verbally operate it." He would tell me, "That is not the kind of switch you have. There's nothing wrong with the switch. The problem is with the way you want to operate it." God wired our wives—correctly I might add. What we have to do is find out what it is what "turns on" a wife when it comes to sexual intimacy. It's not just standing at the foot of the bed yelling, "Turn on!"

Everything I truly understand about a woman could be written on a sheet of paper—and then it still would be blank. Tami has tried to help me understand, and I want to try to be a voice for her and hopefully for your wives regarding this subject, to the best of my ability. Maybe the fact that I like Broadway musicals will help. I don't know.

A husband comes to bed with the anticipation of sex. He expects that his wife is equally as anxious for it. He's got his shoes off and he's ready to go. His wife walks into the room and she's not wearing red, sexy high heels or even a "fun shoe." She's wearing…well, she's wearing house slippers. Not literally, but it is pretty obvious that she's not thinking the same thing that he is. He's frustrated. His wife says, "Well, I'm not in the mood." He may interpret that several ways. The husband may think, *"My wife hates sex or she hates me. She isn't in love with me anymore. I don't think she finds me desirable anymore. Maybe we don't really belong together, because when it comes to sex, we're not on the same page."* All because she said, "I'm not in the mood." Let me see if I can help you better understand better what she's saying. She may be saying, "I'm not in the mood." Yup. That's it. It's not a comment about you or your relationship or how she feels about sex. She's just not in the mood.

I love Mexican food (There's a quick subject change). I could eat Mexican food morning, noon, night, and snack. I call the fourth meal, "Fiesta Siesta." Every once in a while, Tami will say, "Hey, what are you in the mood for tonight?" and I might say, "Oh, some barbecue sounds good." She doesn't respond incredulously, "What? You're not in the mood for Mexican food? You don't like Mexican food anymore? You don't like the way I make Mexican food? You're not eating Mexican food with someone else, are you? I guess we'll never have Mexican food again!" I don't have to explain. She understands that I'm just not in the mood for Mexican food tonight.

Now, I'm not suggesting that your wife is Mexican food, and every once in a while you need to go out for barbecue. What I am saying is that it is possible when you say you are not in the mood for something, it just simply means that—at the moment, you're not in the mood for it! The same is true with your wife and intimacy. It isn't a commentary on intimacy in general. It's not a measure of the status of your relationship. She's just not in the mood. A wife could mean, "Listen, I'm just not in the mood."

Or, she might say, "I'm too tired." Although it might be hard for us to understand, what she may mean when she says this is…well…"I'm too tired." That's it. Have you ever been too tired to do something you really liked to do? I like to golf. In fact, I get my money's worth. A lot of guys are trying to get 70s and 80s in their scores. I'm getting around 110 or 120. I'm measuring it per stroke. I'm getting lots more value out of my golf. There used to be a municipal golf course in Denver that would fill their tee times really quickly. It's a really nice golf course to play. In the summer they would leave a few tee times open on Saturdays for walk-ons. They were given on a first-come, first-served basis. And you could be there really, really early and get in line for one of those. A friend of mine called me and said, "You want to try to walk on tomorrow?" I said, "Sure, what time?" He said, "We probably need to be there about 5:00 a.m." This meant that from where I live, I needed to be up at 4:15 a.m. After a full work week, I didn't want to get up. I could go lose my golf balls in a lake much later in the afternoon.

For those who say, "But don't you just love the sunrise?" My reply is that the sunset looks exactly the same in reverse direction, and it's later in the day. I'm not a morning guy. And there have been times in which I've told my golfing friend, "I am just too tired to golf." It doesn't mean I don't like to golf. It doesn't mean I'll never golf. It doesn't mean I'll never get up early to golf. I'm just too tired to play that day. When a wife tells her husband, "I'm just too tired" regarding sex, it may be because she has been home with your little "angels" all week and she's too tired.

So when she says, "Not tonight." Instead of standing there yelling, "Sex On!," perhaps we husbands might ask ourselves, *"How can I help her?"* Consider how she is wired. What if a husband were to call sometime and say, "Honey, I know it's been a busy week for you. I've called my parents. They're coming by to get the kids after school. Leave the dishes, leave whatever else you have to do today. Take a bubble bath. Take a nice nap. When I come home, I'm going to get you, we're going to go out to dinner, and I've booked us a room at the hotel downtown. We're going to eat, we're going to go there, and spend the evening together. We'll come back and pick up the kids tomorrow." She is going to say, "Oh, I know what you have in mind! Great!" Then there's no need to talk about it, either. You've already figured it out! Sometimes it's just a simple matter of saying, "Can I do something to make the mood better? Can I do something to help so she's not as tired? Can I do something to operate her switch the way in which she's wired?" Because sometimes our wives will come to bed wearing house slippers.

Sometimes she'll come to bed wearing orthopedic shoes (you know, those nurses' shoes that may be great and comfortable to walk in, but there's nothing about them that's sexually attractive? It's just squeak, squeak, squeak, squeak, squeak all the way down the hallway). Again, I'm not talking physical shoes. There are times in a woman's life when, physically, intimacy is not the way we would want it to be. For example, God has designed the reproductive cycle of a woman such that, once a month on the average, she is not—as the old commercial said—at her "freshest." It involves those puffy days in which she is uncomfortable, and she doesn't feel as clean. As men, we are asking, "Well, what's wrong?" and she replies, "It's just not a good time of the month." It might also be during that so called "the change of life" (that's the biggest understatement since Noah said, "It looks like rain") of menopause with its mood swings, hot flashes, the change in personalities at a moment's notice…and oh yeah, a drop in sex drive. It might be during pregnancy. It's in the ninth month. She's tired; she might not feel pretty. She doesn't feel comfortable! She tells her husband, "Not tonight." Her husband explodes, citing the supposed medical and Biblical evidence for her to participate. And he thinks, *"Well! I guess that means it doesn't matter to her anymore. My needs don't matter. Apparently, she doesn't love me. She doesn't see the value of this."* That's not what she said. He's not paying attention to her, just himself. It's just not a good time for her physically.

Not understanding this is like going in, finding your wife cradled over the toilet, throwing up from the flu, and saying, "I guess this means we won't be having sex tonight?" Someone making a statement like that would be uncaring and unthoughtful. There are physical times in a woman's life—whether it's because of health, because of "girl things," because of age—in which she says, "I'm just saying I'm not where I would want to be for intimacy." By the way I've never met a woman that loves those time either. None of them like that their sex drive has tanked. None of them are happy about the physical discomfort because it gives them an excuse to not have sex with their husbands. They dislike it just as much, if not more, than their husbands.

It may very well be that what we're wanting is not the "fun shoes" of sexual intimacy, but the "sexy" stiletto heels of just sex. When our wives don't come to bed wearing those (figuratively or literally), we're disappointed. It may very well be that, as men, we have been sold a bill of goods when it comes to intimacy—we have been told that this is what is "sexy." I don't know if you know this, but Victoria's Secret catalog is not for women. It's for men. Victoria's Secret's approach is this: "Spend $40 on a pair of underwear, then your wife will be sexy." Retailers, the media, and the world are convincing us that high-heel shoes are sexy; lingerie is sexy; something you saw in a movie or read in a magazine—that's "sexy." Men don't buy the *Sports Illustrated* swimsuit edition for the articles. No, it's to look at the pictures of the near-naked ladies. That's what it's for. They get fooled into thinking, *"Oh! That's sexy. That's what I want, need, and must get from my wife!"* She should be wearing sexy shoes all the time.

Whether it is the objectifying of women through pornography or some of those things that we consider to be more casual (though I believe they are just as much pornographic), we require our wives to conform to the unrealistic and corrupted view of what sex and sexy really is. Tami walks in from her bath, wearing multiple glasses, flannel pajamas with stripes going the wrong way, hair kind of dripping, and she is desirable to me. I don't mind her trying to do something "special" for me once in a while, but let's not spend money on something she's not going to wear long. It's just not worth it. She's desirable to me because of who she is to me, not just because of the outward appearance.

With that being said, of course a wife needs to be equally sensitive to her husband's wiring too. I know a woman whose husband was working his way out of a porn addiction. She told me, "I will not dress sexy for my husband because that's how they dress in those porn videos and pictures, and I'm not about to give him the satisfaction of getting what he wants." Did you catch what she said? "I'm not going to give him what he wants." In other words, *"I know what operates his switch, but I'm sure not going to do that."* The pornography was certainly a problem, but so was her attitude. Tami will be sharing more about a man's wiring in the next chapter.

It's really important that we understand the difference between sexual intimacy and intimacy. *Sexual intimacy* refers to the physicality of our relationship and *intimacy* speaks to the relationship itself. Sexual intimacy is one of the ways in which we are connected to one another. It is part of the process of developing true intimacy. But we should not confuse the two. In Genesis 2:24 Moses writes the words of Adam, of God, or his own commentary, "Therefore a man shall leave his father and his mother and hold fast to his wife, and they shall become one flesh." This "one flesh" literally means "mingled or mixed together." In marriage a couple is joined by many things; by agreement, by ceremony, by law, by kids, and by sex. But, the process of becoming one flesh is the process of becoming intertwined with one another. Sex is a step in that process. It is an important step, but it is not the only step. Sex will contribute to real intimacy, but as a relationship grows, many other things will produce this mingling. This is especially true of our wives.

You need to talk with your wife (spouse) about sex. I know, men don't talk about sex. That needs to change. Sex is an important part of marriage. You need to have a dialogue with the person that is in your marriage (that's your spouse). Begin to investigate this by saying, "I don't know, but I'd like to." Make an effort to understand where your spouse is coming from. There are some things that she likes and some things that she doesn't like. There are things that she is comfortable with and things that she is not comfortable with. You as her husband need to know what those things are.

I am aware of a husband and wife, newly married, who were having trouble in the bedroom. He was concerned that there was something wrong with her or something wrong with him or something wrong with them. They went to a marriage counselor, and during their sessions it was discovered that she had been sexually abused by her father, a brother, and an uncle when she was young. Obviously, this had contributed greatly to the problem that they were having. Had they never had a conversation about it, he may have never known where her struggles originated. Once it was discovered, they were well on their way to resolving their issues. A conversation with your wife does not mean that there is some deep seated or traumatic incident in her past. Have some conversations and try to consider her needs, her wants, and her desires.

I asked Tami what are some of the things that a wife is concerned about when it comes to improving a couple's sex life. Some of her answers surprised me. They might surprise you as well. I hope they help you. Here are her thoughts.

"Number one," Tami said, "a wife wants her husband to believe that she is beautiful, all the time. Anytime. Morning, noon, night, and she needs you to tell her." Then I told her, "Fine. Then you tell the wives to quit telling us that they're ugly. Tell them to quit telling us that they're fat. Tell them to quit telling us that they're wrinkled. Wives need to quit telling us that they're old. Because before long, you're going to convince us that you're not very attractive." I went on, telling wives to quit dressing in the bathroom or closet so their husbands can't see them naked. We like seeing them naked, because they are our wives and we think they're beautiful. Now, I'm not asking you men to lie, but you do believe they are beautiful no matter what and they need to know that you do.

"The second thing," she said, "is that your wife wants you to desire **her** and not just sex." Your wife wants you to say, "I want sex **with you**—and it's only with you that I'm going to find satisfaction." You can have sex outside of your marriage relationship and find a degree of satisfaction. But I am convinced, because I know how God designed us, that you will never find the full fulfillment in intimacy outside of the marriage relationship, ever. I don't care if she's great. I don't care if she's beautiful. I don't care if she just a dynamo. It doesn't matter. God designed intimacy to work perfectly in marriage. And anything outside of that is not going to be perfect even if, for a time, you think it is. Your wife needs to know that you want her. You want and desire her, and no one else.

Tami continued, "She needs to be free of distractions." I asked her what she meant by distractions. The conversation went something like this:

Her: "Well, you remember when we moved into the prison apartment?"

Me: "Yeah."

Her: "Do you remember when we were there?"

Me: "Yeah."

Her: "Do you remember when my parents came to visit for the first time?"

Me: "Yeah."

Her: "Do you remember how the walls were like an inch thick?"

Me: "Uh-huh." (I still wasn't getting it)

Her: "That's a distraction. I am not going to feel extremely amorous when my parents are in the very next room."

Me: "Oh yeah."

She went on, "Do you remember that time that one of the kids had a nightmare on a Friday night, and rather than getting your lazy tail out of the bed to tuck him in again, you just said, 'Hey, get up in bed with Daddy?' Saturday morning, you were feeling a little frisky, but the baby was still in the bed. That's a distraction. Do you remember when we were having all kinds of money troubles? Do you remember when we had screamed and yelled at each other at dinner time? Do you remember when we were worried about this or worried about that? Those are distractions."

The way women are wired, they need to be free of some of those distractions. And if there's a way that we men can help with that, then help.

Then she said, "A woman likes a little romance." This is where I put up the stop sign. "Enough," I said. "I'm tired of hearing about romance. We are fix-it guys. You know, 'Here is a hammer; here is a nail.' I can fix what needs to be fixed—just tell me what tools I need! You want me to hold your hand? Say, 'I like it when you hold my hand.' Great—I'll hold your hand. Say 'I like it when you put your arm around me at church.' Great—I will put my arm around you at church. You want something? Fine. Just tell me."

Bottom line, most husbands have no idea what a wife means when she says, "romance." So Tami clarified, "Your wife might like to wake up one morning after you've gone to work and find a sticky note on the mirror that says, *"I love you"* or maybe another idea is to put something in my Bible where I do my daily Bible reading, where I've got my marker for the next day. If I open it up and there's a little note that says, *"I am so glad that I have a godly wife...."* It didn't stop there. "And you know, every once in a while, I would like us to go out to eat without the kids" (note the change from "them" to "us").

She said, "Then, I thought maybe we could perhaps have some conversation." I said, "You mean like talking? On what subject?" "About anything," she said. "We could just visit. 'How was your day; how was my day?' or 'What movies have you wanted to see? What's going on in the world?' We could just talk." I replied, "You mean like through the whole thing?" (I have purposefully left out her response to my response). She went on, "Then, maybe you could bring a single rose home. Surprise me with it and just lay it on the counter for no reason whatsoever." Bonus tip: Young men, don't buy a dozen roses for your girlfriend. Start with a carnation. Build your way up. I have found that, when positioned correctly, a single rose can be far more powerful. The unexpected is powerful!

That's quite a list: "Leave a note. Go out to eat. Nice music. Have a conversation. Surprise me…." Is that **all** really needed to get your involvement? I'm only human. Really it does not take this long or a difficult list. She was just reminding me that a woman is wired differently than a man. She needs to be romanced, wooed, given your undivided attention. Remember, for her it is more about the relationship than it will be the actual physical act of sex. That doesn't mean she doesn't enjoy the physical act of sex, but it begins in her head not in her body. We don't understand it. It's not the way that we're wired. But we need to work harder at trying to understand them.

She added, "Your wife might like you to be clean." Hygiene may not mean the same to a man as it does to a woman. You might show up after you've just finished mowing the yard, with your hat hair and a brown strip around the elastic of your underwear because you have sweated, and stand there saying, "I don't know if you know this, but it's Friday night…." Apparently that image of the muscular farmhand coming in from shoveling hay saying, "Ma'am, is there anything else you need?" only works if you look like Brad Pitt. A wife wants you to take time for a little bit of hygiene. Brush your teeth. Take a shower. She puts clean sheets on the bed; act like you like clean as well.

She went on (I know. I asked). "Wives would like their husbands to be more interested in giving during intimacy than in getting from intimacy." In other words, think more about her than you do about you.

After hearing her list of demands…uh…I mean suggestions…I felt that I needed to simplify it into one single statement to share with husbands. I came up with, "Instead of trying to get your wife into sexy shoes, try sweeping her off her feet." It is poignant and poetic. I felt that summarized it perfectly. Then one day I picked up my notes to find that Tammy had written underneath that summary, "And you might be very, very, very glad that you did." Her point? When we begin to see intimacy from our wives' perspective, understanding how they are wired to some degree and trying to take that into account, we will also benefit. Our wives now become an integral part of the same process—at the same time they become interested in how we are wired, what we like, and what we want.

That's where intimacy grows into a relationship. I believe that intimacy is an important part of a marriage relationship, but I am equally convinced that it is not the most important. Because in all likelihood, the day will come when intimacy will fall out of fashion. Maybe for a day, maybe for a week, maybe for a whole lot longer. And a relationship that has built itself only on sexual intimacy will fail. A marriage is benefitted by sexual intimacy, but when intimacy falls out of fashion or it isn't what it once was, the marriage isn't over. Don't think there is nothing more to value within that marriage. When a relationship is being built on more than just sex, there is something far more sustaining—far more fulfilling—that remains.

CHAPTER 9

THE FASHION OF PASSION: INTIMACY IN MARRIAGE (FROM A WIFE)

The more Wayne and I travel, meeting people going through marriage and talking to people about marriage, the more we see that problems with intimacy are real. And I do think it's because we don't talk about it in the church. We've let the world make it something dirty and ugly. There are so many women within the church who see it that way. They see sex as something you **have** to do. Some see it as something repulsive and they don't understand why it's there—it's a "man thing." But that's not right! We need to be more open about how beautiful sex can be within marriage. Intimacy—sex—should be talked about in the church. Okay, probably not to the two-year-old class, but we should be teaching about it. It was designed by God to be a beautiful blessing in marriage, to both the husband **and** the wife.

When I was first married and read books on marriage that would describe the needs of the wife and the needs of the husband, I soon realized that most books didn't really work for me. I fit the **man's** description and Wayne was the **girl**. In fact at first I thought there may be something wrong with me. Maybe I wasn't being the Christian woman I was supposed to be, Maybe I hadn't pushed out my "sinful self." I am the more sexually aggressive one in our relationship, and Wayne is the one with the interest level more often attributed to women. I soon learned that there was nothing wrong with me; Wayne and I were just wired differently. That's the case in most marriages. God may have designed us that way to keep us from staying in bed all of the time. It doesn't mean that one is right and one is wrong; we're just different.

Wayne is the only man with whom I discussed this lesson. I didn't talk to other men and get their opinions on intimacy. That's much too personal! In fact, I would ask you to be very careful of whom you talk to regarding your sexual relationship. I know that I've talked about it with friends before and unknowingly painted a picture of my husband that was not healthy for other women to have of him. If they are not getting that kind of relationship at home, these conversations can possibly begin planting seeds of discontent in their minds or in yours. Just be very careful.

I want to start out by giving us a Biblical foundation. God is the one who designed us to be sexual in nature. It is a God-given thing. It is part of who we are. It goes back to Adam and Eve. God created Adam, and He parades the animals by, but there is no one for Adam. So, God makes woman, a female for Adam. If He just wanted to give Adam a companion, He would have created another man or he could have a dog for a companion. But it was more than that. He created someone with whom Adam could reproduce. Reproduction is certainly part of the relationship. But there have been times in which, because it was taboo to talk about sex, generations and generations of women lived with a stigma, an understanding, pressed upon them that "it's just for having children."

That's not all that it is! We learn from reading 1 Corinthians that the Christians in Corinth had asked some questions about sexual relationships. Paul responded with this epistle. In 1 Corinthians 7:1-9, he gave direct answers to those specific questions. He starts in verse 1, saying, "Now concerning the things about which you wrote, it is good for a man not to touch a woman; but because of immoralities, let each man have his own wife, and let each woman have her own husband. Let the husband fulfill his duty to his wife, and likewise [*likewise* means in the same way] in the same way also the wife to her husband. The wife does not have authority over her own body, but the husband does; and likewise, or in the same way, also the husband does not have authority over his own body, but the wife does. Stop depriving one another, except by agreement for a time that you may devote yourselves to prayer, and come together again, lest Satan tempt you because of your lack of self-control. But this I say by way of concession, not of command. Yet I wish that all men were even as I myself am."

Paul never married. Paul was single. But he understood that not everyone should or could live that way. "However, each man has his own gift from God, one in this manner, another in that, but I say to the unmarried and to the widows that it is good for them to remain even as I, [which is single] but if they do not have self-control, let them marry; for it is better to marry than to burn." Remember, the church in Corinth is highly Gentile and they are coming in with their "idol worship" thinking. Temple prostitutes were a part of that thinking. Paul is going to answer their questions in a way to convey that most people are going to have this desire in them, and each person's spouse is intended to fulfill that desire. He wanted them to know that it was not a sinful desire that they have when it is fulfilled in marriage. We need to talk about it within the church the way it is meant to be discussed, as something beautiful within marriage.

Intimacy is a gift you save for your marriage. When you do that, what a blessing it is to give this gift. It's a benefit you receive when you're married. Start teaching that to your teens—they will have a better appreciation of the purity they can carry into their marriages, instead of wondering why nobody talks about it and indulging that curiosity. We plant that seed of curiosity by never talking about it, never conveying how beautiful it is. But we can't do this until we ourselves start to see it as something beautiful, something that belongs in marriage.

I am going to share with you some thoughts that men would like for you to know where intimacy is concerned. I want to take you back to the wedding day. There is the groom in his shiny rented dress shoes at the front of the auditorium, waiting for the bride to appear. The bride is thinking, *"I can't wait for him to see me in this dress. My hair is amazing; my makeup is great. I've spent hours picking out the perfect wedding gown, I've picked all of the colors, I've picked all of the flowers; everything is perfect."* And when those doors swing open, I can almost guarantee you that when the groom looks up, his eyes are full of tears. He is thinking, *"Oh, she looks like a princess in that dress...."*

And in the back of his head he is thinking, *"And I can't wait to see her panties."*

I say that because one of my sons shared that with me. It was definitely T.M.I. I had just said, "Oh, her dress was so pretty. She just was so beautiful. Didn't you think her dress was gorgeous?" "Oh, yeah," he said, "but you should have seen her panties." I did not need to know that! But I had raised him as a godly man, and he was excited about that part of his married life. *"Well,"* I thought, *"good for you, son. Good for you."* This is how men think!

As we talk about sex, I'm not talking down about men. Men are usually wired different than we are. While women need to be **fed** on the inside, men need to be shown that you love them through physical behavior. It is the physical that speaks to men. It is the physical that fulfills their needs. For women usually, needs are met differently. "Tell me how much you love me. Show me that you love me by picking up your socks. Show me that you love me by speaking gently to me." So, it can be difficult for us to understand the sexual needs of the relationship sometimes. Women often think, *"What is the big deal? I just don't get it."*

In fact, I would describe my wiring like the male I just described. I came into this marriage relationship as one of those people who need physical affirmation to let me know that I am loved.

It's not fair to think that someone who is not wired like you is wrong. I want to make sure that you are working to build a healthy sex life within your marriage while you can. Is it the most important thing? No. But is it important? Yes, because it is part of God's design for marriage.

First, I want to encourage you to express yourself where intimacy is concerned. I don't know why we think when we put two young people in a marriage bed they're going to know what they're doing sexually. They're not going to know anything! If you take a godly young couple and bring them into a marriage, you don't want them "learning" about sexuality from movies. You don't want them reading up on it from secular sources. We don't want them learning that way! Or even if you're both older and coming into a second marriage, he doesn't know what needs **you** have. Understanding the intimate relationship comes from communicating with each other. That can even be difficult within marriage sometimes because it is embarrassing, it is personal, and we have been programmed not to talk about it. Regardless, your husband is wanting to be this manly man even in the marriage bed. It's one more realm in which he may be saying, "I don't know. I don't know what to do. I don't know what you like, and I don't know what to do for you." They would fall over if you said, "Let me show you." This is one area to learn to express yourself. It's okay! You're in your marriage bed where God intended for it to be. Communicate about your intimate relationship. I don't care how long you've been married, the intimate relationship you have with your spouse changes. We've been married 40 years, and it has changed all along the journey. Just when you have your mind wrapped around what works, life throws you a doozy, and you rework everything—even your intimate relationship. This is one area in your marriage that requires communication. You should be communicating in all aspects of your marriage, but your husband wants to hear from you regarding your intimate relationship as well!

Here is something else to consider. If you aren't the sexually aggressive one, you need to be that for your husband sometimes. Wayne and I are different and I learned that right from the beginning. Wayne and I got married, spent the night in Wichita, then we lived with his parents for a week. My thinking was, *"We're married now, we're in bed together, we should be naked, having sex!"* The first time Wayne and I did not have sex during that week, I cried. I rolled over in bed and did that silent cry. *"Great,"* I thought. *"We've been married—two days, three days—and he already doesn't find me desirable."* Wayne put his hand on me and whispered, "Are you crying?" I had to tell him why I was crying. "It's only been 3 days and already you don't find me desirable." Wayne replied with, "Tami, we're in my parents' home; this is awkward." But it didn't take me very long to realize that we aren't sexually wired the same. He was the person with a headache or too tired.

In the early part of our marriage, the heating and air conditioning years, that difference in our wiring made me defensive. It hurt me and instead of talking to him about it, my personality being what it is, I pushed him away. I thought, *"Fine. You want any of this you can come to me."* I thought, *"When he is in the mood, he'll let me know."* I was hateful.

One day, Wayne came to me and said, "Tam, I need to talk to you about something." Those are never good words. I said, "Okay, what is it?" He said, "Do you not find me desirable anymore?" Because of the way I think and the way I am wired, I thought, *"Duh! Yeah, you know who I am."* "What are you talking about?" I asked. And he said, "I cannot remember the last time you made a move on me or tried to seduce me." That defensive part of my brain wanted to say, "Well, you want to know why, Mr. Headache, Mr. Too Tired?" And I had to stop myself. *"Okay, wait,"* I thought. I couldn't think of the last time that I had, so I had to explain why. He said, "You always used to be right there. I guess I've treated you bad." And he apologized. He said, "I didn't realize what I'd done, but it made me feel like you don't find me desirable anymore." Sometimes the wife needs to be the initiator. We may be thinking, *"He's the one that wants it; he'll let me know when he wants it."* But they want us to put the moves on them sometimes, too. It makes them feel wanted and desirable.

Now, I'm a person with a small frame. I was blessed by a little, bitty grandma, and I've always been very self-conscious about my body. When we were married, I had no curves. I bought my bras in the teen section (and it was usually in the preteen sizes), because I had no curves. If I wanted curves, I had to buy them. That was my figure. I was a bit self-conscious on my wedding night. Wayne made me feel desirable, and I have moved past that. But then I entered into another phase of life, within the last few years, where I now have curves…just not where I want them. Don't you wish we could take the extra curve in our thighs and push it up into our bras? There was another occasion on which Wayne came to me, saying, "Tam, we need to talk." And I'm thinking, *"Oh, what have I done now?"* He said, "I never see you naked anymore." And I thought, *"Why would you want to?"* I told him I didn't understand what he was saying. He was being dead serious, and he told me, "I'm a godly man. And you are the only one who I will ever see naked. And if I don't ever see you naked, you're pushing me in the path of sin." I had never thought of it that way! Satan has given him the ability, through his cell phone, in the very palm of his hand, to see a naked woman. I don't want that for my husband; I want it to be me!

I had to be more deliberate about my routine. Our schedule was that I would go take my bath, then get out of the tub, putting on flannel jammies to hang around in for the rest of the evening (or, shorts and a T-shirt, depending on the time of year), and then when midnight would strike, I would go to the bedroom, put on my nightgown and climb in bed. By the time he came out of the bathroom, I was already in bed. Next morning, I would get up and go to the bathroom. When I came out, he would get in shower. While he was in the shower I got dressed. Our paths were not crossing! I didn't realize he wasn't seeing me naked. I hadn't thought about that! I had to be deliberate, delaying the routine a little every now and then so he was getting to see me naked. It was so uncomfortable—and this was a man I'd been married to for years! I'd hear him coming up the stairs and I would have to stop myself, take my time and make sure he saw me naked. We want them to be godly men. Especially if you've been married a few years, you may be thinking, *"Oh, I hate it. Why would he want to see this old body anymore?"* But your husband needs to see something naked, and you're his only option. Remember that and flash him once in a while!

Another thing to remember on this journey of marriage is to flirt with your husband. Flirt with him! Just like you did when you were trying to get his attention in the first place. Let him know you think he's cute. Wayne is such a goofball. Once he had gone to get a haircut, and when he came home, I was working at the kitchen table on a lesson of some kind. He came in the door, and we were chatting, but I was still kind of distracted. I finally realized that he was still standing there, so I looked up and asked, "Are you alright? What's going on?" He said, "What do you think of my hair?" All I could think was, *"You're such a girl!"* But I stopped, looked at him, and let him know, "Well, she did really good over your ears...." What do you say to a man who has gotten his hair cut the same way for 58 years? It made me realize that he wanted to be told that he's attractive. I had to take a moment and tell him, "Oh, you look so nice!" And I have to continue to throw that out every now and then. Make sure that you flirt with the man! Tell him. "Oh, I love your eyes in that blue shirt" or "I love it when you wear clean jeans." He wants to hear from you.

We need to recognize that, especially if they are striving to be like Jesus, somebody will be flirting with our godly men—even within the church. A several years ago, a friend of mine was at one point obviously flirting with Wayne. I finally pulled her aside and (I told you, I'm a very vocal person) I said to her, "I'm watching you flirt with Wayne and you have to stop it. You're flirting with my man." I tried to be nice about it. Well, her eyes filled with tears, and she started telling me about her marriage. Her husband wasn't raised in the church, he was a new Christian, and he wasn't yet being who God wanted him to be. He wasn't being who she thought he should be. And she said, "I look at you and Wayne, and Wayne's just got it all together." I reassured her and we prayed together. I told her that I understood but reminded her **not** to flirt with him anymore.

So be aware; there will be women flirting with your husband, even if you're not. Men can be so naive; I told Wayne, "She was flirting with you!" "She was just being nice," he replied. "No, she was flirting with you." Sometimes they just don't know. Men need to be lifted up. They need someone to flirt with them. We think we're the only ones who feel that way, but they do as well. So, flirt with your husband!

Next, never, ever, ever withhold sex as a punishment. We females are powerful creatures…very powerful! We use sex as one of our super-powers. It's having the attitude of "You made me mad, and I will show you!" Beware of this attitude, and never, **never** withhold sex as a punishment. That is not okay! Or if he is the sexually aggressive one and you aren't, be careful of shutting him out, thinking, *"No one needs sex that much."* We know that withholding sex is not something God takes lightly. In 1 Corinthians 7:5, it says, "Stop depriving one another except by agreement for a time that you may devote yourselves to prayer." The only time you do not come together is when you purposefully set yourselves aside for spiritual reasons. I had a gorgeous young woman point out to me that she was wired along the same lines as I am, and she mentioned that Scripture. She told me that she had to let her husband know that she was unintentionally turning the heads of other men and it was as if he was throwing her in the path of Satan by shutting her out because sex wasn't important to him. I hadn't really thought of it in those terms. But it says you come together lest Satan tempt you because of your lack of self-control. When you withhold sex from your spouse, it's like you're throwing him out there, saying, "Satan, come get him. I'm not going to fulfill his needs. Let's see how long he can go." You have to be so careful, because Satan is saying, "Oh, good. I know he needs that, and you're not going to give it to him so we will just start parading some women by that might give it to him." Don't be naive. Just because you're in the church, don't think it doesn't happen. I am watching so many marriages fall apart because of unfaithfulness, because of adultery. And often it's because of the attitude that says, "I don't want to give that to him"—either because I'm angry or just simply because I'm not sexually wired in the same way. Just be aware of this behavior in your life.

Now, I call this next section, "When Passion Isn't in Fashion." I have five children and this sexually aggressive woman had her moments of tiredness as well. I did daycare in my home for years to help bring some money in. Well, I can remember one Friday evening during the heating and air conditioning years, Wayne came home and had that twinkle in his eye. You know the one. He'd say, "Hey, it's the weekend." Twinkle, twinkle. I had all of those little ones—I'd have a baby on my leg and vomit on my shoulder. I couldn't remember when the last time I washed my hair. And I'd be looking at him asking, "Now? Now you're ready? Now you want that?" And in my head I'm thinking, *Oh, I'm so tired. I'm so tired.* Sometimes it's the last thing on your mind. Wayne and I were going through this part of our marriage in which I was tired, and he was tired, and life was just so busy. We were picking each other apart. We really weren't being very nice to each other. We realized that we had pushed our sex life out of the picture. And when I am not sexually fulfilled, I start getting a little testy.

This will sound kind of pathetic, but we made a decision and it worked for us. We started scheduling our sex night. I know it sounds sad. We decided Friday night would be it. That way, we could both wrap our heads around it beforehand. I'd have all day Friday to be preparing my mindset. I could take a shower, I would wash my hair, whatever it might be, to have myself ready for *Friday*. On Friday mornings I could drop a note in Wayne's lunch or pocket with something seductive written on it and it helped him set his mind that direction as well. It made a huge difference in our lives! It really helped us not lose that God-given blessing in our marriage because we were too tired and distracted at that point. I can still text him even on a Wednesday and say, "It's Friday." His response might be, "Maybe tomorrow," or "Woo-hoo!" and then I know where I stand. But sometimes you have to purposefully put it in your life or it gets lost.

Different phases of life can also present a hindrance in your intimate life. It may be pregnancy, or health issues, or body changes. Mine is hormonal. I never gained weight in my life. I would have a baby and walk out of the hospital weighing the same thing I weighed when I conceived. I am blessed; I get that. Well, now, I've started gaining weight. And I found myself sharing things with Wayne, such as, "Look, Wayne! Look at this thigh. Do you see this? It's like somebody poured gravel under my skin! Do you see that? That's so gross!" Or it would be, "Look, I have absolutely zero muscle. Have you ever seen an arm do that before? Remember when my muscle used to go up on my arm instead of dangle here beneath?" Or I'd grab that band of excess flesh around my middle and say, "This must be what they're talking about when they say muffin top. But I'd say this is more like a bundt cake." I'd be going on like this, and Wayne finally said, "You have got to stop talking like that. Tami, that's disgusting and if you keep doing that, I'm going to start seeing you as disgusting." And I'm thinking, *"Oh, that wasn't my intention. That's bad!"*

Why do we do that? As women, we are so hard on ourselves. We are always pointing out our flaws, even to each other. If I compliment a woman by saying, "You look great in that dress." The response is usually something negative, "This old thing?" or "Do you think it makes my behind look big?" Because we've got the world telling us what our shape should look like and what the perfect form is. God has created us each different on purpose and He hasn't created anything that isn't beautiful in His eyes.

Now, if you need to do something to improve your health, go do that. We need to be taking care of our temples so that we can serve others better. But if you just don't think you have the perfect size, you're going to have to let it go. Pay attention to how many negative things you say about yourself. It's something we do, and we should be careful of that. Don't talk about yourself in a disgusting manner, because then your husband will start seeing you that way. He doesn't want to think like that, because he loves you and he sees you as this beautiful person! Wayne suggested that I, "Start thinking sexy thoughts." Now I know that *sexy* is a worldly word, but we're talking about godly marriages. He said, "Start thinking that way about yourself. Start thinking beautiful thoughts. Remember that's how I see you. I think you're hot. I think you're sexy."

I shared this at one of our first seminars, and a few weeks later one of my more voluptuous friends came up to me and said, "I've got to tell you my story about your *sexy thinking* point." I'm thinking, *"No, please keep it to yourself."* They had been to the seminar and one night when she went to bed there was this silver lingerie lying across the bed. "All I could think was, 'I'm going to look like a sausage in that,'" she said. "I was so disgusted, thinking of myself appearing in front of him in that nightgown." But she thought, *"Okay now, I can do this. He bought it for me. He wants to see me in it. Tami told me I can do this."* So, she put it on, looked at herself in the mirror, and started telling herself, "Okay, he thinks I'm hot. He thinks I'm sexy. He thinks I'm beautiful." She repeated it to herself a few times and before long she kicked that bathroom door open and went out full of confidence thinking, *"He thinks I'm hot! He thinks I'm sexy! He thinks I'm beautiful!"* "It worked," she said. "He was blown away!" It worked! So, if you need to, think sexy thoughts. We need to think that way, remembering that they see us as beautiful! They love us.

We need to be careful also of being in a rut kind of attitude. It's really easy to start taking your sex life for granted. We had all of these little kids, and I was trying to make sure that my husband's life was not becoming the "same old, same old" thing. Back in the heating and air conditioning years I would hear all of the young couples around me say things like, "We're going to the mountains for the weekend." Or, "We're having a get-away, just the two of us." Well, I'm looking at my kids, thinking, *"Nobody babysits five kids overnight (and if they do, I have to untie them the next morning and let them go)."* That just wasn't going to happen, so I had to think outside of the box.

It was our camping years and we had this three-bedroom tent. One Friday night, I went out into the backyard and set up the tent. I made a little fire pit, I hung lanterns in the tree and made a nice bed in the tent. I tried to think like Wayne and scattered rose petals all around the tent. When Wayne came home from work, he noticed the tent set up in the backyard and asked what was going on. I told him that we were going to have a get-away, just the two of us. He asked, "What are we doing with the kids?" I told him, "We're going to lock them in the house." We had those latches on the front door that you could latch up high (because our kids would try to escape—there were times I'd purposefully leave them unlocked, but most of the time I'd lock them). I knew that if they wanted out of the house, they'd have to come out the back door and we would be right there. I could hear them if something happened. We had a getaway together in the backyard! Wayne was blown away! So sometimes it helps just thinking outside of the box. Try being the initiator. Don't sit back thinking, *"He's never taken me anywhere. We've never done an overnight in a hotel. He's never done anything special for me."* What have you done for him? Do that a few times and see what happens!

Now let me encourage you to make sure that you always think any idea through. Wayne's always doing something special for me. He's so thoughtful. For example, I had been away to speak at a retreat, and when I came home, he had done all of these wonderful things. Well, one night during the ministry years I thought, *"Okay, I'll do something nice for him."* He had been away speaking at a teen retreat all weekend and I knew he would be worn out. I saw a commercial for a hot rock massage and decided that would be perfect. I thought, *"I'm not paying money for it though. I can do this!"* I went over to a park and found some smooth river rocks. I brought them home, washed them all up, and I heated them in the microwave (which I found out could make them explode—it could have been very dangerous, but I didn't know that. And mine didn't). I laid the blankets on the bed so that I could do this little hot rock massage when he came home. I lit candles and had the whole romantic vibe going on. I sent the kids to a movie or something. When he got home, I told him that I had a special surprise for him—I was going to give him a massage. He was so impressed! He went and got ready and laid down on the bed while I got everything ready.

I remembered at the last minute that I didn't have any kind of massage oil. I knew I had vegetable oil or suntan oil, so I went with the suntan oil because it smelled better. I reheated my rocks and was ready to go. I got the oil, squirted it on his back and rubbed it around. Then I picked up one of those hot rocks. Well, those rocks were **really** hot! And my hand was all slimy, so when I picked up the rock, it went *kerplop* on his back. It was really hot! He screamed and arched his back. I was trying to slap the rock away, but I was laughing so hard that it took me a minute or two. I share this to say that sometimes thinking outside the box is not the best way to go. That story is one of my favorites, because I thought, *"I'm going to do something so special for him,"* and it left a red mark on his back. Just make sure you think it all the way through.

We want to make sure that we are taking care of our intimate relationship while we can. Because there may be a time coming when it isn't a part of your relationship. It may be pregnancy; it might be health. There may be a time coming when it's not a part of your life at all.

For me, right now, in this hormonal/non-hormonal, menopausal stage of life, my libido has crashed. I have Wayne looking at me and asking, "You still find me desirable, right?" My response is, "I have no idea. I think so. I have no idea what's happening inside my body. But I do love you." So while you can, make sure that you are working to build a healthy sex life. Because I know that if you go through hard things in your life, your intimate relationship can pull you back together.

I understand if unfaithfulness occurs, such as pornography or even adultery, whatever it might be—if your husband has been unfaithful, the natural response might be, "Fine. You wanted that, go have that, you're not ever having me again." Or, if you have been unfaithful, you may be thinking, *"Why would he ever want me? Why would you ever want me again? How will that ever happen?"* I'm here to tell you that over time, the sexual relationship can actually help heal a marriage. It is going to take time. But part of the healing process is coming back together and letting God use that physical element to heal your marriage and bring you back together. My experience is that Satan gets his foot in the door with unfaithfulness, but we don't want to let him to ruin everything. My thinking is, *"Okay, you may have gotten that, but you're not getting my marriage!"* We need to be intentionally fighting for our marriages. It takes time and it takes patience, but we need to be working to save our marriages.

I'm looking down the road to the phase of marriage that I'll call sexy Orthopedic Shoes, and I know those words don't seem to go together. It's the phase that we understand that it's not all about the sex. We know that sex is a benefit that we receive in marriage. A benefit that we get while we can.

I call it sexy orthopedic shoes because of a mental picture that I have of my parents. (Relax!) I go and stay every year for a week with my parents in Oklahoma. It's just Mom and Dad and me. I love my time with them! They are so cute together. I get goofy from my mom. I love my mom to death! Now, my mom can sing, and I mean sing beautifully. But she seldom sings normal around the house. She just sings in kind of an operatic, off key voice. So, Mom will be puttering around, singing in the kitchen, just being silly. And my dad will be sitting over in his chair, and he'll have his Bible or his newspaper, and I can just see him looking up over the top of his Bible, and he'll say, "Isn't she beautiful?" And he'll have this little twinkle in his eye. And I'm looking, thinking, *"Well, yeah. I think she's beautiful. She's my mother."* But I watch my dad, and I see those expressions. He looks at my mom and he doesn't see her outer self—he sees the beautiful woman that she is on the inside. And it's because she's renewed herself day by day. One of my favorite scriptures is 2 Corinthians 4:16, "Therefore we do not lose heart, but though the outer man is decaying [and it is! TR], yet our inner man is being renewed day by day." She's striving to look like Jesus, and they've built a wonderful relationship. Have they fought for their marriage? Sure—we all do!

That's what I want in my marriage! When Wayne looks at me, I don't want him to be focused on my outer body because this old thing is starting to fall apart. I want him to look at me and think I'm beautiful because he sees Jesus in me.

My prayer is that, as you go back into day-to-day living, you will remember that marriage is a blessing. Strive for a marriage that glorifies God. You can only control you. So day by day, work to renew. And don't be too hard on yourselves! Just take it one moment at a time and do what you can to be more like Jesus. Lift your husbands up! They are so different than we are. Be patient with them, and they'll come around. Remember, God's in charge. I have seen Him work miracles in the lives of people.

Your marriage will be beautiful because you're striving to be that godly woman. That's who your husband's going to see. He's going to see the inside. When he looks at you, he's going to say, "Man, she's trying so hard. She's striving. Oh, she's so beautiful!" And he's going to look at you and instead of seeing Orthopedic Shoes, he'll say, "I see Stilettos. That's who I see."

We want marriages that stand strong. We're going to have struggles, and we're not always who we're supposed to be. That's okay. Just strive! We make mistakes, but we get back up and we try again. Hang in there!

- Sit down together and talk about the positive aspects of your sex life. I know it can be uncomfortable but do it anyway!

- Make sure your husband sees you naked every day. You may have to send him a picture to accomplish this. Be careful!

- Tell your spouse what you like best about his body. This can actually be seductive. It may start with his eyes, but let him know what about him stirs you.

- Get out the lingerie. Or garter belt. Whatever! Plan a night of seduction. (Let me discourage a hot rock massage.)

CHAPTER 10

KEEPING YOUR SHOES SHINED: FAITHFULNESS IN MARRIAGE

You guys might find it interesting why it is that you have remained faithful to your wives for so long. Here is a list of reasons from a magazine article that I read. It's entitled, "Men Who Don't Cheat." What caught my attention was that it featured a picture of some celebrities, all of whom have been married to one person for a very long time. Andy Garcia, Dan Akroyd, Spike Lee, Alice Cooper, Kevin Bacon, along with Alan Alda, a guy that is pretty left in his thinking (from my perspective) and not a spiritual, religious guy. They've all been married to one spouse. I wondered what the secret was for these high-profile individuals who work in an industry where marriages are frequently discarded. But it turned out that this article really wasn't about them, it was about you, about me…about us. You might like to know, according to the article, why it is **you** don't cheat on your spouse. These are the reasons the writer gives:

First of all, you don't cheat on your spouse because you're apparently "too lazy." It's not that you don't want to cheat on your spouse. But you would much rather stay home, watching the ballgame and eating popcorn than get up and get yourself a girlfriend. The one that you have right now waits on you hand and foot, so why mess with another one? Or it may not be that. Perhaps it is the second reason offered: you are "incredibly ugly." You were fortunate to get the gal that you have. You'd get another girl, but nobody would have you. I mean, even a pork chop around your neck would not make the dogs like you anymore. Reason number three given suggests it is because you are "cheap." So, you're not only lazy and ugly, but you're a cheapskate. And having an affair costs money. I mean, there are dinners and roses and cards and all those things that you did when you were courting your wife—not to mention secret getaway spots are just too expensive for you. Then there was this one, "Bores can't get dates." So, if you didn't feel bad enough that you're lazy, cheap, and ugly, you're also a boring person. Nobody would have you. How your wife can stand you is amazing. The article offered a couple more possible reason for your faithfulness: you have the fear of getting caught (so, you're a chicken on top of everything else) or affairs are time-consuming. I mean, at some point having a mistress just becomes another job to keep, and your to-do list is already too long.

The reasons given in the article may have been offered in jest, but I don't believe them to be true in the least. I believe that men are faithful because they are men of character who keep their promises and that women are faithful to their husbands because they too made a commitment. In other words, it is an admirable characteristic that, even if things aren't perfect, you recognize that there's something above and beyond that. Something that drives you to say, "We're going to stay in the same house together, even if it's in opposite ends of it." That isn't the best arrangement, but there is something to be said for sticking with it no matter what.

Everybody recognizes that "unfaithfulness" is a sign of flawed character. That's why is it all over the tabloids? *"So and so was last seen at some nightclub with So and so, who is not his wife."* It's why everybody talks about it when they find out that some "pastor" in their community has been having an affair? In a world in which people change spouses almost as if it were the same as changing shirts, why is it that people bother to say, "They're having an affair"? I mean, we even had a president that looked squarely into the eyes of the American people and denied it (lied) when many Americans were doing the same thing. They were up in arms, even some who were his biggest fans. Why? Because they saw it as an issue of overall character. Deep down inside, we all know unfaithfulness isn't right. People don't see it and say, "You know what? There's a really good man of character. I know that because he's unfaithful to his wife." Or "she really shows her character in her unfaithfulness." No. We recognize that there is nothing admirable about unfaithfulness.

Well, when it comes to marriage, unfaithfulness is more than just undesirable. It's destructive and can be devastating. Tami and I have experienced its destructive effect firsthand in our own family. It was devastating to everyone involved.

This is typically where even the casual observer says, "Amen. Unfaithfulness in marriage is destructive and adultery will destroy a marriage." Christians add, "There is no doubt that sexual unfaithfulness is a sin before God, that it will be punished by God if not corrected." Admirably, most couples recognize this and make the commitment, "That will never happen to us!" I pray that's true. However, I'd like to suggest that unfaithfulness comes in ways other than just in the sexual unfaithfulness of adultery. In fact, there may be unfaithfulness in your house right now. It may even be that you are the guilty party, and you don't even know it. I fear that while we guard the front door of our marriage from sexual unfaithfulness, we leave the back door open to other forms of unfaithfulness that can be just as destructive. I'm talking about those things that we don't think about as being unfaithfulness. In and of themselves, they are not all sinful, but they lead us in a path of unfaithfulness where something or someone else has replaced our spouses, filling the role or taking time and attention that should belong to our spouses. I've tried to boil them down to a few key categories.

FRIENDS/FAMILY UNFAITHFULNESS

Tami and I have a close friend who discovered that their father had been carrying on a number of affairs for several years. He and his wife at the time had been married for almost 60 years. When he was approached on the subject, he said, "There is no inappropriate activity going on with these women. This is not a sexual relationship. We don't hug, we don't kiss, we don't hold hands. I just like spending time with her in conversation. We have coffee, and we just do stuff together. We're just friends. That's all it is. This is not unfaithfulness." I doubt that any reasonable person would agree with him that this kind of involvement with a woman who wasn't his wife was "just fine" since it never became sexual. I think it's important to note that he refused to stop the behavior, and it ultimately resulted in a divorce. After that, one of these "just friends" became his second wife.

When another person begins to take the place of your spouse in conversation, in friendship, or in companionship, you have crossed the line into unfaithfulness. But it doesn't just have to be with somebody of the opposite sex. It is possible for us to be unfaithful with someone of the same sex. There are some ladies who have found their women's meeting, their PTA group, even their ladies' Bible study group to be where they would rather spend their time. Because "There, they understand me, and there we can talk about these kinds of things. My husband just isn't able to fulfill that for me." They prefer to gather with or vacation with or spend time with these other women. The husband is replaced by friends.

Gentlemen, this may be unsettling to you, but you may be one who is unfaithful to your wife with the guys with who you golf with, or bowl with, or hunt with, or just hang out with. When your perspective is, "I would much rather spend time with these guys. We have a great time together," your wife is neglected. Now there is nothing wrong with having friends. It's all right to have friends. It's all right for married couples to have individual friends and friends together. It's all right to spend time with friends even if your spouse isn't always included. It's all right to have friends of the same sex and the opposite sex. Let me pause here to remind you that friends of the opposite sex can be dangerous territory for married individuals. Those relationships must be marked by respectful boundaries and intentional action to avoid an inappropriate relationship. Even in the absence of inappropriate behavior or sexual unfaithfulness, unfaithfulness occurs where companionship and conversation with your spouse is being substituted by someone else.

It's not limited to friends either; your spouse can also be replaced by family. (I suppose they are friends too, or at least I hope so). Your kids, your parents, your in-laws, and your siblings are very important, but they cannot be allowed to take the place of your spouse. Children, especially when they are young can be a drain on your time and energy, but don't let them take so much of your time and energy that you don't have any left for your spouse. You were partners before you were parents. You need to stay partners. Mothers can be a great resource for their married daughters and fathers a guide for their sons. Their relationship with their children will probably never be as rich as when those children are grown. But mommas and daddies shouldn't take the place of best friend, nor should they be allowed to get between a wife and her husband. "A man should leave his father and his mother and shall cleave to his wife" (Genesis 2:24). The same is true for wives. Family is a wonderful thing, but the most important family member is your spouse.

ELECTRONIC UNFAITHFULNESS

If you were to ask Tami who my best friend was, she might jokingly say (at least I hope she's kidding), "His phone." I guess she would say that because it's with me when I wake up and when I go to bed. It's with me most of the day. I talk to it a lot. We have become quite the pair. You see my phone will answer a question day or night. She'll play music for me. She'll search the internet for all kinds of information. She's always very polite to me. I could even change a setting and give her an Australian accent if I wanted. Oh yeah, when you ask my phone, "Siri, what is my name?" She says, "Your name is Wayne, but because we are friends, I get to call you 'Your Majesty'." I like that. That's comforting. Did you notice that I even call her a she? Well, she may be a problem, an unfaithfulness problem. But I mean, who doesn't love their phone? We have probably all seen a whole family sitting around the table at a restaurant (or our own kitchen) and everybody's on their phone. There is virtually no conversation among them. And if there is, it's only via a text.

If we're not careful our electronics can become our very best friend. During a break at one of our seminars I had a man who had been married more than 50 years come to me, saying, "I wish you'd spend more time on that electronic unfaithfulness, because my wife is in love with Candy Crush." I laughed. Then I realized he wasn't laughing. He went on to say, "When we go to bed, she's playing Candy Crush. When I wake up, she's playing Candy Crush. When we're around the dinner table, she's playing Candy Crush. When we're in the car, she's playing Candy Crush." He reiterated, "My wife is in love with Candy

Crush" and he added, "We rarely ever speak." He felt she had abandoned their relationship for a new electronic best friend. Our phones, tablets, computers, televisions, and gaming systems can take an unhealthy place in our lives and be destructive to our marriages. For more information on how technology is damaging not only our marriage relationships, but our relationships in general, check out the book *Disconnect* by Jeremy Roberts. (Yes, he's our son.)

Electronic unfaithfulness has exploded in recent years via social media and opened the door to another danger: private messaging that allows us to communicate with anyone, virtually anywhere, anonymously. Some of those conversations should not ever take place. We have Facebook, and within Facebook we have PM's or "Private Messenger." We have private text messages or emails that can be sent. Maybe you have heard about the phone app Snapchat (or something similar) in which a man or a woman can send a picture of anything. Yup! **Anything**! When they send it and it's opened, it supposedly remains open for only a few seconds. It then vanishes for good, or so they thought. Young men and young women found out they could take a screen capture of it on their phone, save it, forward it to friends, or to anyone…or everyone. That's not really the problem I'm talking about.

On the one hand, these private messages may be funny pictures or harmless conversations and not all inappropriate in their content, but are they appropriate? Is it appropriate for a spouse to have a "private" conversation without their spouse's knowledge? The answer? No. At our house we have a rule that if Tami or I are texting or messaging someone of the opposite sex, we have to include the other one in the text. There's never a chance for questions to arise. This practice occasionally is a burden, however. We have some close married friends that we used to spend a lot of time with. Tami sometimes texted all of us and said, "Would you guys like to do dinner on Friday night?" If she included any of the men in the text, she included me as well. What followed would be two hours of my phone blowing up while the ladies chit-chatted back and forth, "Yep," "K," "Time?" "6," etc., etc. I'm thinking, *"I don't care who you talk to, what you talk about—just get me out of that circle, and let me know at the end of it."* But you know what? I don't have to worry about inappropriate things ever being talked about. Additionally, our computers and phones are fully accessible to the other person, anytime. A preacher friend of mine always reminds folks, "If you are having to delete texts, messages, or emails so your spouse doesn't see them, then you shouldn't be sending them."

PORNOGRAPHIC UNFAITHFULNESS

The familiarity and the advancements in technology have brought pornography into our homes and hands. Gone are the days when someone would have to ask the 7-Eleven cashier for those "dirty" magazines behind the counter or go to some seedy bookstore to obtain it. Young men, young women, old men, old women, and everybody in between—anyone is able to view pornography. It is now available 24/7 from your phone, tablet, television, and computer virtually anywhere you are.

Before we go on, let me just say this as a sidebar to the discussion of marriage (though I suppose it needs to put in the spotlight to show its ugliness). If you view pornography, you need to find some help to get it out of your life. There is nothing good for you in it. It will not only destroy your marriage; it will destroy you. There is no redeeming value in pornography. Not only does God describe this kind of immorality as sinful, but statistics bear out the devastating affect pornography on all aspects of life. It is destructive emotionally, financially, socially, and relationally. With that being said, let's move on.

Pornography is a plague; it is a sin and it most certainly is unfaithfulness. Remember we have defined "unfaithfulness" as anything that takes time or attention from our spouse that was due them. Pornography certainly does that, even if it does not result in an act of sexual infidelity. It isn't adultery but it is still unfaithfulness. This is where somebody asks (although it rarely comes out as a question), "Well…um…I caught my husband looking at porn and…uh…in Matthew 5, Jesus said if a man looks at porn on the internet and lusts, he has committed adultery. So that means I can divorce him and get another husband. Right?" I certainly believe that her husband shouldn't be viewing pornography and I want to be sensitive to their situation and feelings, but I typically will answer something like, "Well, is that what you're looking for, a way to get rid of your husband? Or are you looking for a way to save your marriage?" Because those are two different approaches. That typically is not the answer that they want to hear. But their question regarding Matthew 5 does help in our understanding of the relationship between pornography and unfaithfulness. Here's what Jesus actually said, "You have heard that it was said, 'You shall not commit adultery', but I say to you that everyone who looks on a woman to lust for her has committed adultery with her already in his heart." Pornography is most certainly is a sin, because it is sexual immorality. But the lustful looking is not adultery in a literal sense. We know this because in the very same context, Jesus says that if you hate your brother, you have committed murder in your heart. No one is calling for anyone who has been hating someone else to be arrested and incarcerated for the crime of murder. Adultery is when a desire is actually acted upon, not the desire itself. Pornography is lust—it is sin, and it is unfaithfulness. But in the sense that the word *adultery* is used, it is not that. At the same time, just like hating someone can lead to causing them harm, lust is a desire that can lead to acting on those desires. Jesus' point is this: Faithfulness is a heart matter and so is unfaithfulness. By the time it has already visible outwardly, it has been sitting in the heart.

One more word about pornography and its damaging effects. For a long time, pornography and porn addiction has been a chain hung around the necks of men. But, ladies, our world is changing and pornography has its hooks into women as well. A survey a couple of years ago showed that 30% of 3000 women surveyed viewed porn at least once a week and another 30% at least once a month. Another survey, with similar results, reported that 87% of Christian women have viewed pornography, 17% weekly and 7% multiple times a week. Unfortunately all those statistics are on an exponential rise.

Part of the reason is that pornography has been rebranded as "romance." Referred to by some as "mommy porn," it's finding its way into mainstream acceptance through films like *Fifty Shades of Grey* and so-called "romance" novels that pervert and twist sexual activity and the relationship between a man and a woman. These volumes are not being bought by seedy, twisted, weird, perverted individuals. They are being bought by mothers with small children. In fact, *Fifty Shades* replaced the Gideon Bible in some hotels in New York and in California because it is what women would prefer to read. I could say a whole lot more, but I think the point is made. Porn is no good for your marriage.

WHAT MIGHT HAVE BEEN/WHAT MIGHT BE UNFAITHFULNESS

This is when one spouse thinks (or fantasizes), *"Oh, if I had married him/was married to her, my life would be so much better."* It's filled with thoughts like, *"They understand me," "They wouldn't treat me the way my spouse treats me,"* or *"They are _____ (insert some superior and exaggerated characteristic)."* This unfaithfulness—and it is unfaithfulness—is based in fortune telling because it is certainly not based in reality. It's feelings not facts. It's a man who is looking at a woman at his work, or a neighbor or a friend, and wondering, "What would it be like…?" It's a woman who looks at her kid's soccer coach, or a guy at church, or who is living a life inside her romance novel and imagining something better than life with her husband. It's "the grass over there is always greener" perspective. Well, the grass over there may be greener, but it still has to be mowed. It may not be as green as you think either. The reason that the grass under your feet seems dead in comparison may be because you have not been tending your own yard. It may be that the reason that other person is so "understanding" is because he doesn't have to live with you and the reason you find her so wonderful is you are not having to live with her. Maybe? You need to recognize that none of us can tell the future. It may be that a relationship with another wouldn't look much different than the one you are in, because **you** would still be in it. If you are the one pondering this imaginary life, you're the unfaithful spouse! (I know; that thought might sting a bit). Additionally, this fantasy land of thought leads to further dissatisfaction in your marriage because no real-life spouse can ever compete with an imaginary one.

If you really want to imagine something, imagine that your spouse is being unfaithful. Imagine that he spends his time thinking about someone else and how wonderful it would be to be married to her and not you. Imagine you come home from work or school and you find a pair of shoes under your bed that don't belong to you or your spouse. You begin to ask about it. Before long, it is revealed that he or she has been having an affair. Even worse, imagine finding your spouse in the bed with someone else. How would you feel? How would you feel about being the one that's left out of a relationship? Would you feel happy, relieved, angry, betrayed, devastated, etc.? Would you say, "This really made my day" or "This has ruined my life"? Would it make you feel better about yourself and better about your spouse? Or would it all be horrible? What would it be like to be the person who is not the "guilty party"? Start thinking about that. It's not so interesting to fantasize about, is it?

Faithfulness is a deliberate choice and action to keep the marriage bed pure (Hebrews 13:4). But it's not just the bed. It's not just about sexual intimacy. It is about our relationship. It's a **full** commitment to the individual to whom you are married. It's keeping the promise **you** made on your wedding day. Faithfulness says, "I am committed to **this** individual."

I hope you're are beginning to think a little bit differently about unfaithfulness— not just about the morality of it, but also about the various forms in which it comes. Unfaithfulness is anything that has replaced our spouses, filling the role that they are to have in our lives or taking the time or attention that should be given to them. Unfaithfulness of any kind is bad. It is bad because it's destructive to a marriage. It's bad because in time it will ultimately destroy a marriage. It is bad because it can become a sinful practice that could cost us our souls.

One final thought. What about when unfaithfulness occurs? Can a couple reconcile and can that marriage be restored? The answer to both of those questions is, "**Yes!**" I know a man and his wife whom I appreciate greatly—a wonderful couple. They were both great workers in the kingdom and admired by everybody. He was in a terrible automobile accident, and while he was hospitalized, one of the men of the congregation came to comfort my friend's wife. Unfortunately, things became too "comfortable," and they engaged in an illicit sexual relationship. In time it came out about the affair. I'm sure everybody thought: *"This will be devastating! They won't be able to stay at their current church because of the embarrassment. It's going to ruin her reputation. It's going to ruin this man's life. They'll never survive this. They'll never have the same influence in the* *kingdom that they once had."* But they did survive. In fact, their relationship was restored. They didn't just restore the marriage. They restored their reputation. They stayed at the same church. They returned back to kingdom work. Today they are both respected by those who knew them before the affair and by those who know nothing of the affair. In fact, if I told you the name of the couple and you knew them, you'd think, *"No way. Not them! They are a model married couple."* They found reconciliation when the woman came forward, repented her sin, and asked for her husband's forgiveness. He forgave her, and in time trust was restored and faithfulness returned. It didn't come easy, but it can happen. Unfaithfulness can be resolved, and beyond that, a marriage can blossom again.

And if you're one of those people who says, "Ah, it'll never happen to us" without taking any intentional steps to prevent it, you are foolish. Unfaithfulness comes in all shapes and sizes. It is not only sexual infidelity. It might not start out as sinful but can lead to sin. Unfaithfulness in one way or another always destroys—always. It never is a good thing for a marriage. But, unfaithfulness does not have to be the end of a marriage. It is something from which you can recover but it's going to require some time, some work, and certainly God's help.

HIS SHOES HER SHOES: SOLE MATES

CHAPTER 11

IT'S ALL ABOUT THEIR SOLES (SOULS): GETTING TO HEAVEN... TOGETHER

It was 1971. A man by the name of Bill Bowerman was serving as the track and field coach for the University of Oregon. Bowerman was having a struggle. Several of the universities had been introducing new synthetic running tracks at their facilities, and Bowerman's team, simply put, was not performing very well. They were still using the old traditional metal spikes, and this caused a problem. Bowerman began to consider ways to help his athletes perform at their very best on those additional track surfaces. One morning his wife made him waffles for breakfast. He saw her working, and he suddenly he had "a revelation," as he described it. He grabbed the waffle iron. He ran to his workshop in his garage and dumped some kind of rubber goo into the waffle iron. When it cooled, he peeled it out and stuck it to the bottom of a track shoe. The Nike waffle sole was born. The rest, as they say, is history. About 10 years ago, some renovations were happening in Bowerman's backyard, and they dug up the very waffle iron with some other junk Bowerman had buried out behind his workshop. This was Nike's "Holy Grail." The waffle iron is now safe and sound in Nike's archives. It is rusted and ruined. It doesn't work and can't be repaired. It will never make another waffle. However, it isn't really about the waffle iron; it was about the sole. A few years back, Nike introduced a new reengineered waffle sole. I was watching a little documentary about it, and one of engineers said, "Well, you know, when it comes to Nike, it has always been about the sole." At that moment something hit me (maybe because about that time I had been thinking of nothing but shoe illustrations for our seminars).

Marriage is all about the "soul." God is the designer of marriage. He had some pretty grand purposes behind His design: companionship, partnership, parenting (not just reproduction), etc. I also think marriage has a lot to do with understanding our spiritual relationship with God and is a benefit to our spiritual well-being. God is interested in more than just your happiness. He has something bigger in mind. God is not concerned merely about your "happily ever after;" He is infinitely more concerned about your "happily **forever** after." It's about the souls of the people in that marriage. It has a benefit for their souls and the souls around it. At the same time, the condition of our souls has a great deal to do with the condition of our marriages. Marriage is all about the soul, and your soul has a lot to do with your marriage.

Let's look at this a little closer. When I say marriage has a lot to do with your soul, I mean this: God created us as intimate sexual beings and He provided an avenue by which we can express that intimacy in the marriage relationship. That relationship is much more than biology. The sexual relationship between a husband and a wife is quite different, far more complicated and far more fulfilling than the "birds do it, bees do it" of the animal kingdom. In 2 Corinthians 7, the apostle Paul wrote to the church in Corinth speaking about the value of intimacy to a husband and wife.

> The husband must fulfill his duty to his wife, and likewise the wife also to her husband. The wife does not have authority over her own body, but the husband does; and likewise the husband also does not have authority over his own body, but the wife does. Stop depriving one another.... (1 Corinthians 7:3-5)

Paul doesn't mean that we own our spouses. He means that we are designed and created for our spouses. He intends for us to complete and complement our spouses. Intimacy practiced in any other way would be empty and ultimately unfulfilling. So, God calls sex outside of the marriage sinful, because it would go against His intent and our well-being. We have the desire, and that desire has an outlet. Marriage allows us the free and guiltless expression of that desire.

But it's really even more than that. Marriage is not only is about keeping us from sin; marriage gives each spouse a partner who can help them in their spiritual walk. Think about it men. Would you be much of a leader if you kept your wife fed, kept her in a nice house, and made sure she always had everything that she needed—but never helped her in her journey towards an eternity with God? What kind of leader would you be? Wives, what kind of a helper or a helpmeet would you be? How would you be that support that Tami talked about earlier if you were just the maid, the nurse, even someone who waited on your husband hand and foot, demonstrating submissiveness in every possible way—but you never helped him in his walk to eternity? Would you really consider yourself to be a success? I don't think so. In other words, God has blessed us in our marriage relationships with someone who is helping us, a Sole-Mate, one who is concerned about our souls above everything else.

However, it's not just about **our** souls. It's about the souls of the children we may have. Sometime back, I heard somebody say, "Oh, that church over there, they're not very big on evangelism. All they ever do is baptize their children." *"Well done,"* I thought. In an age in which so many children are leaving the faith of their fathers, it is good to know that there are people who believe, "We have been entrusted specifically with the souls of our children, and we're going to guide them to God." Now, we know that there's a lost world out there, and we do want to go into all the world. But would we consider ourselves to be evangelistic successes if we converted everybody on our streets, yet our children abandoned the faith? Marriage is also all about their souls as we partner together with that goal in mind.

It's not just about the souls of each spouse and the children; it's about the souls of those people out there in the world. It's often said of preachers that they live in a glass bowl and someone is always watching them. Well, I have news for you. There is somebody watching you, too. You just don't know it. There is a neighbor, a friend, or a family member. There are others who are watching you to see how it looks to live out Christianity. There are people who are looking at your marriage and saying, "What is it about them that is so different? How do they survive every crisis? How have they stayed faithful to each other in a faithless world?" Your marriage answers, "Because we trust in God and seek to be faithful to Him." Your marriage is a sermon about love, sacrifice, and faithfulness to God as you show your love, sacrifice, and faithfulness in your marriage. If you're not letting your marriage be all it's supposed to be, you may very well have unknowingly endangered someone who is following after you. So it's also about their souls too. We have this great opportunity in which God says, "I am concerned with your soul and the souls of others, and I have given you the blessing of marriage to help you and to be a shining light to those who are around you."

Not only is marriage about the condition of our souls; our souls have a great deal to do with the condition of our marriages. In other words, the better our spiritual walk is, the better our marriage walk is and when our spiritual walk struggles, so do our marriages. Marriage has to be consistent with our overall life goal to bring glory to God. It is why we were created in the first place. It's why God takes care of us. It is the reason that God sent Jesus to save us, that we would bring Him the glory that He deserves. If we are to bring glory to God with our lives, then guess what, we're going to have to do it in our thoughts, in our actions, in our jobs, in our activities, in our relationships, **and in our marriages**. Everything we do should bring glory to God. You see, there is no glory given to God in disobedience. For us to pursue a marriage pattern or objective different than what God has instructed dishonors Him. Any truly successful marriage relationship will have as its ultimate goal to bring glory to God. It needs to fulfill His will and purposes. It's not just about "what I want" or "what she wants," or kids, or happiness, or sex, or companionship. Marriage is about God's plan for us! God did not grant us life so we could get through marriage. He gave us marriage to help us get through life. When a marriage pulls us away from God's plan, when our commitment even to our spouses takes us away from our commitment to God, guess what? It's not the kind of marriage God wants.

God detests unfaithfulness in a marriage. It's reminiscent of how unfaithful humanity has been in general. I think it's why God often uses marriage terminology when He talks to His children who had rejected Him. He calls them "adulterous" people. In marriage, we are given such a wonderful thing. When we're unfaithful, I know God thinks, "You can't even be faithful with this little thing I have given you! You are unfaithful in the small things and the big things." In the end, it's all about faithfulness to the end. It's about faithfulness to our spouses and faithfulness to God.

When a couple struggles in their relationship and they want to fix that, the place to begin is the soul. What we have to do is make sure we fix the hole in our souls before we try to fix the holes in our relationship. My dad had a pair of leather dress shoes that he took in to be repaired. It was around 1980, and I would guess he probably paid as much as $75 for them. Now, that may not be considered a high-end shoe these days, but in 1980 it was a pretty high-end shoe. My dad always wore a hole where he rocked on the balls of his feet. He took them in one day to have them resoled. The guy wanted something like $35 or $40 to resole the shoe! When we came back out of his shop, I said, "Dad, the shoes were $75, why didn't you just buy a new pair of shoes? Why would you resole old shoes?" He said, "Because they're good shoes, and they're worth saving." The same is true with your marriage. It may be "old" (or old fashioned) and may show the scuffs and scrapes of walking life's path, but your marriage is good and it's worth saving. Sometimes it just needs "resouling." Here are some ways to resoul your marriage:

SPEND TIME IN GOD'S WORD TOGETHER

I know many people who are, individually, great Bible students. They do daily Bible reading, Bible marking, and personal study. Tami and I each have our individual study projects. For her it's preparing for a retreat, Ladies' Day, or Bible class. For me it's a sermon, class, or other teaching opportunity. But it is something extra special when Tami and I get to work on the same thing together. Perhaps it's working through a passage of Scripture independently, sharing what we've learned, and then suddenly we begin to discuss, study, and work together. We see things we had never seen before as the other points to things in the passage. For example, preparing the material for our seminars is this way. We are able to work together, we look at God's Word together, and it helps us see God's plan for us as a couple. Not just a plan for Wayne or a plan for Tami, but a plan for Wayne and Tami. Spend some time in God's Word.

SPEND TIME IN PRAYER TOGETHER

We need to kneel in prayer and humble ourselves before God, call upon Him for strength and help. It's when we say, "We've got holes in our souls. We need Your help to shape us, mold us, and guide us."

SPEND TIME IN KINGDOM SERVICE TOGETHER

It is unfortunate when I hear people say, "Well, we cannot attend that particular church event," or "We cannot be involved in that particular ministry because we really need some family time," or "We've just been really busy, and that's a lot for our family." There is no better "family time" then time spent as a couple or family in kingdom service. I know, decorating for Vacation Bible School may not sound as good as a Disney cruise to the Bahamas. I know because I've done both. But I can tell you right now that a family will be better blessed by time spent in kingdom work than they will be on any vacation. The vacation will pass then it will be nothing more than a memory, and they'll just wish for the next one. But when time is spent in kingdom service, it has eternal benefits. It will always strengthen your marriage and family. Take your place as a team in the kingdom.

In the Nike shoe documentary I mentioned earlier in this chapter, the shoe engineer not only said, "When it comes to Nike, it's all about the sole," but also said, "It is where we have come from, and it is most certainly where we are going. It is all about the sole." Well, I'm convinced that when it comes to marriage, it's just the same way. It is where we have come from—meaning, it is out of a marriage relationship that most of us were born. It also has a great deal to do with where we're going and where we'll be forever. Marriage is a great blessing to the soul, and a strong spiritual walk is a blessing to the marriage. And truly, if there is nothing else that you take away from this book, keeping those two principles in your mind and pursuing them diligently will make your marriage not just survive but thrive!

Hopefully, what we have shared in this book has realigned you to a truth you already knew. There may not have been any real revelation that made you commit yourselves to working harder at your relationship. But that's alright. Sometimes it's a reminder of the commitment you made to each other and to God on your wedding day that is all that you need. If there was something special that you never have thought of before, or something that gave you a new perspective on your marriage or your spouse, then our work has not been in vain. You have sacrificed your time to read and consider our thoughts; we pray that it has not been time wasted and that God will bless you and your marriage.

HIS SHOES HER SHOES: SOLE MATES